PRICK

CACTI AND SUCCULENTS: CHOOSING, STYLING, CARING

PRICK

CACTI AND SUCCULENTS: CHOOSING, STYLING, CARING

GYNELLE LEON

MITCHELL BEAZLEY

For Petrona x

An Hachette UK Company
www.hachette.co.uk

First published in Great Britain in 2017 by Mitchell
Beazley, a division of Octopus Publishing Group Ltd,
Carmelite House, 50 Victoria Embankment,
London EC4Y 0DZ
www.octopusbooks.co.uk
www.octopusbooksusa.com

Distributed in the US by Hachette Book Group,
1290 Avenue of the Americas, 4th and 5th Floors,
New York, NY 10104

Distributed in Canada by Canadian Manda Group,
664 Annette St., Toronto, Ontario, Canada M6S 2C8

ISBN 978-1-78472-367-5

A CIP catalogue record for this book is available from
the British Library.

Printed and bound in China.

10 9 8 7 6 5

Commissioning Editor: Joe Cottington
Art Director: Yasia Williams-Leedham
Senior Editor: Leanne Bryan
Designers: Geoff Fennell and Ella Mclean
Copy Editor: Helen Ridge
Photographer: Gynelle Leon
Picture Research Manager: Giulia Hetherington
Senior Production Controller: Allison Gonsalves

CONTENTS

INTRODUCTION

In July 2016, I opened the doors to Prick, my boutique dedicated to cacti and other succulents. Based in Dalston, east London, the shop offers a selection of the most unusual and exotic succulent plants, sourced from countries around the world.

I'm often asked why I limit myself to just cacti and succulents, and my answer is always, "Why not?" Once you start to explore their incredible diversity – size, shape, flowers and character – I feel that the question can answer itself. I am constantly amazed by their ability to survive the harshest environments, which makes them a beautiful symbol of endurance and strength.

I've always seen cacti and succulents as living sculptures that take years to develop fully. They are an attractive and sustainable way to transform any interior, and due to their low maintenance and hardy nature, they're well suited to modern city living.

Most people know very little about these wonderful plants, being familiar only with those they've seen in Westerns or the limited range on sale at their local florist or garden centre, and are unaware of the many thousands of species that exist.

My interest in them started with a trip to Morocco in 2011. I visited Yves Saint Laurent's Jardin Majorelle, in Marrakech, and fell in love with the huge cacti and succulents growing in the beautifully landscaped gardens, made even more spectacular by the contrasting vivid blue of the YSL house. I came home

and immediately bought a 1.5-m (5-ft) *Euphorbia candelabrum*. Since then, I've just been adding to my collection.

Not long after, I attended the Chelsea Flower Show in London and saw some incredible flowering cacti on display. I just couldn't believe how many beautiful and unusual cacti existed. I fell in love instantly and had to have them all, but the long distance from my home to the nurseries selling the plants meant that I would have to wait for the following year's show before I could stock up on the most alluring and unusual cultivars.

I created an indoor jungle in my apartment, as I didn't have a garden, but I was growing frustrated at not being able to find locally the unusual large or rare plants that I wanted – there wasn't a single shop in London that specialized in cacti and succulents – so I decided that I would open one myself. It would be called Prick – obviously. I was absolutely passionate about the idea and loved the plants enough to sell my home and give up my job to achieve my dream.

People always ask me where I find my plants and I say from everywhere – and that's the truth. I travel to nurseries all over Europe looking for that special something, and I also visit private collectors. I'm a bit like an antiques dealer, I suppose, but in rare, strange and beautiful plants.

I hope that, with this book, I can share some of that enthusiasm with you.

AUTHOR'S NOTE

This book, which features my favourite cacti and succulents, is a beginner's guide and by no means a definitive publication. I have tried to streamline the horticultural information I've given because much of it is unnecessary for all but the most hardcore fans. I've outlined the key and most interesting facts – scientific and common names, natural habitat, characteristics and care – which, I hope, will increase your knowledge and interest in these plants, and help you to use them to transform your home or workplace, or both.

Sometimes, I've included entries not only on specific plants, but also on the wider genus – the group of closely related plants – that they belong to. This is because I think these whole groups are worthy of closer inspection, either because they're especially popular, or because they contain a whole range of plant species that are great for bringing into the home or work space. Or just because they're particular favourites of mine!

ENDURING POPULARITY

It may seem as though cacti and succulents
have just become popular additions to
the home all of a sudden – and there is
definitely a resurgence of interest in this
historically fascinating and much-studied
group of plants – but they're actually far
from being a new trend. There was huge
interest in them at the end of the 15th
century, when explorers stumbled across
them, then again at the beginning of the
20th century, and again in the 1970s.
I believe their current popularity is down
to a combination of several social changes
and trends.

An increasing number of us live in small
apartments with limited or no outdoor
space. With space inside the home at a
premium, it's hard to devote much of it
to potted plants, meaning that miniature
species are a much more viable way of
building a plant collection.

Busy lifestyles and frequent travelling leave
little time to care for plants, and cacti and
succulents are the perfect solution. They
are undemanding – their natural hardiness
and an infrequent need for watering mean
that they effectively thrive on a certain
level of neglect.

Sustainability is very important to our
generation, with most of us wanting to
waste less, recycle more and be kinder

to the earth. As succulents last longer than cut flowers or other short-term houseplants, as well as needing little water, they are seen as a very sustainable option for adding green to the home.

And, of course, our sense of wellbeing has been proven to increase just by looking at plants, and who doesn't want to feel less stressed and calmer at home? Cacti and succulents are a hassle-free short cut to achieving this.

The popularity of such websites as Pinterest has made us all more aware and appreciative of interior design. Cacti and succulents have enormous artistic value in the home. With their fascinating shapes and structures, they can double up as living sculptures.

Busy lifestyles and frequent travelling leave little time to care for plants, and cacti and succulents are the perfect solution.

DEFINITIONS

In botany, the term "succulent" refers to those plants that have, over time, undergone modifications to their shape and structure, usually as a result of the environment in which they live, in order to help them retain water and survive arid conditions. These modifications have resulted in a huge number of weird and wonderful plants that are not only tough but also simple to grow. It is easy to understand why they are so popular.

Such modifications are many and varied, but they can include:

• **Thick, succulent and fleshy tissue.** This can be seen in the stem (as in most cacti), the leaf (best illustrated in *Lithops* – see page 116) or the roots.

• **Small leaves or a complete absence of them.** Reducing the surface area of the plant cuts down on water loss.

• **Specialized photosynthesis, or CAM (Crassulacean Acid Metabolism).** Most plants open their stomata to absorb carbon dioxide (CO_2) during the day when the sun is out. However, succulents open their stomata at night when the temperature is lower and the air humidity higher, thereby reducing water loss. At night they absorb CO_2 and release oxygen, storing the CO_2 and using it to photosynthesize during daylight hours.

The word cactus is derived from the Greek word *kaktos*, meaning a kind of prickly plant.

• **Spines and hairs.** These offer protective shading. Spines also act as "dew points", ensuring that dewdrops fall onto the soil so that the plant's root system can absorb the water. They also protect the plant's water supplies from animal predators. Spines vary wildly in size, form, arrangement and colour.

• **Wide-spreading roots.** Many cacti and succulents spread their roots over a large area to absorb the maximum amount of water. The shape of the plant often directs any moisture from dew, fog or rainfall down towards these roots to ensure maximum absorption.

Cacti are included in the group of plants referred to as succulents, but they possess characteristics that render them distinct. In the words of cactus expert Gordon Rowley, "All cacti are succulents but not all succulents are cacti."

The word cactus is derived from the Greek word *kaktos*, meaning a kind of prickly plant. The American botanists Nathaniel Lord Britton and Joseph Nelson Rose referred to them as: "Perennial, succulent plants, various in habitat, mostly very spiny, characterized by specialized organs termed areoles."

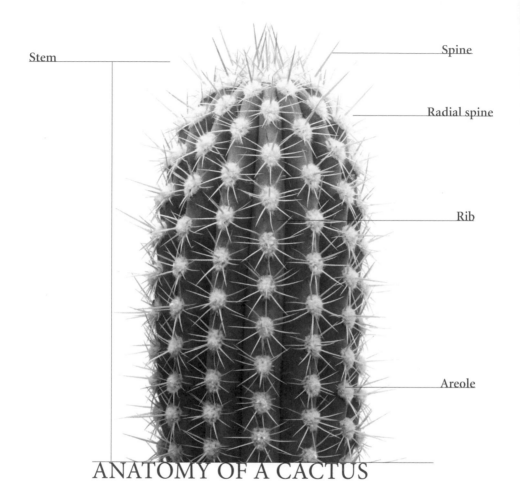

Stem

Spine

Radial spine

Rib

Areole

ANATOMY OF A CACTUS

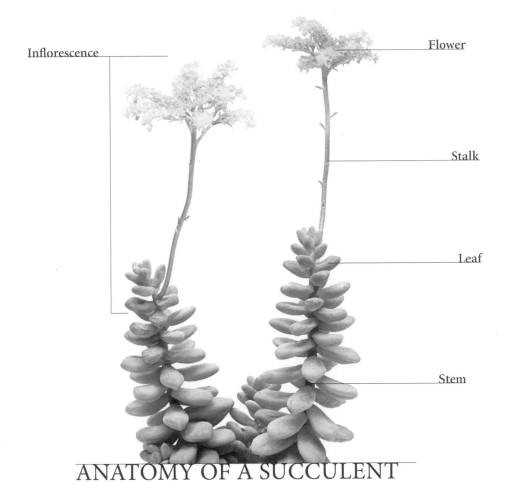

Inflorescence

Flower

Stalk

Leaf

Stem

ANATOMY OF A SUCCULENT

HISTORY & ORIGINS

HISTORY & ORIGINS

Succulents originate from the Old World (mainly Southern Africa and other parts of the continent), while cacti hail from the New World (South and Central America).

The depiction of a succulent (believed to be *Kalanchoe citrina*) on the wall of the Festival Hall of the Ancient Egyptian Pharaoh Thutmose III in Luxor suggests that these plants have been a source of wonder and intrigue for a very long time.

In their native environments, these plants were exploited by locals for their medicinal attributes. It was only in the 15th century, when succulents were "discovered" by Europeans, that they were marvelled at for their ornamental qualities (as depicted in Lucas van Valckenborch's painting, seen here, entitled *Spring, 1595*). When taken back to Europe, these new-found treasures immediately became status symbols, collected by the wealthy and even royalty. Over time, their popularity has grown immensely, to the extent that there are now more than 300 species of cacti cultivated as ornamentals.

It was only in the 15th century
that succulents were "discovered"
by Europeans.

CULTURE & SYMBOLISM

Cacti and succulents represent protection and strength, presumably because of their hardiness, and also wealth. The *Sansevieria* plant, for example, is considered a symbol of protection in its native Nigeria, as well as in Brazil and Korea. Meanwhile, *Crassula ovata* is regarded as a good-luck plant in China, and believed to bring wealth and success.

Sempervivum tectorum has been known to man for thousands of years, attracting many common names, including Jupiter's eye and thunder plant. This alludes to the belief that this plant guards against thunderstorms – *tectorum* is Latin for "of roofs", referring to the traditional place used for growing these plants as a protection against thunderstorms.

Crassula ovata is regarded as a good-luck plant in China.

HALLUCINOGENS

Many people throughout history have regarded certain succulent plants as divine gifts from God. One such example is *Lophophora williamsii* (below), more commonly known as peyote, hikuli and mescal button. This small, spineless, globose plant has psychoactive properties similar to LSD when ingested, and a history of being used for meditation and communication with the spirit world, not to mention pain relief. *Echinopsis pachanoi*, also known as the San Pedro cactus, contains psychoactive ingredients too and is used in a similar way to peyote.

MEDICINAL USE

There is evidence of succulents, particularly *Aloe vera* and *Euphorbia*, being exploited for their medicinal properties as early as around 470 BC. *Aloe vera* (right) was used as a laxative and also to soothe burns and minor wounds. Euphorbias contain a white sap called latex, which, although poisonous, was used to purge, or cleanse, the system, giving birth to the plant's common name, spurge.

FOOD

Many cacti – or, at least, parts of them – can be eaten. One notable example is the edible prickly pear, *Opuntia ficus-indica*, the pads of which are edible, along with the fruit. *Stenocereus thurberi* (organ pipe cactus) produces dragon fruit; *Carnegiea gigantea* saguaro fruit; and *Epiphyllum anguliger* (fishbone cactus) gooseberry-like fruit. *Agave* has been a part of the Mexican diet for over 9,000 years, both as a sweetener and a source of alcohol (tequila and mezcal). The succulent, which has anti-inflammatory properties, can be ingested as well as applied to the skin.

Aloe vera was used as a laxative and also to soothe burns and minor wounds.

PLANT GALLERY & DIRECTORY

INTRODUCTION

There are thousands of cacti and other succulent plants, so I've limited myself here to some of the most interesting and attractive, which, of course, include my personal favourites. All of them will make perfect additions to the home.

Included in my description of each plant, I've given some basic growing information and any interesting facts, and also featured a photograph, which mostly shows a young specimen.

I've also delved into the etymology of these plants, explaining the origin of their botanical and common names. Botanical names are made up of two parts: the first is the genus, the second is the species, which can also be followed by a subspecies. These terms are explained in a little more detail in the Glossary (see pages 214–215).

Over the years, many succulents have been reclassified after DNA sequencing or been given different names by different people. For the most part, I have chosen to give their most well-known names here, but have also included any widely used synonyms and common names, to help with identification.

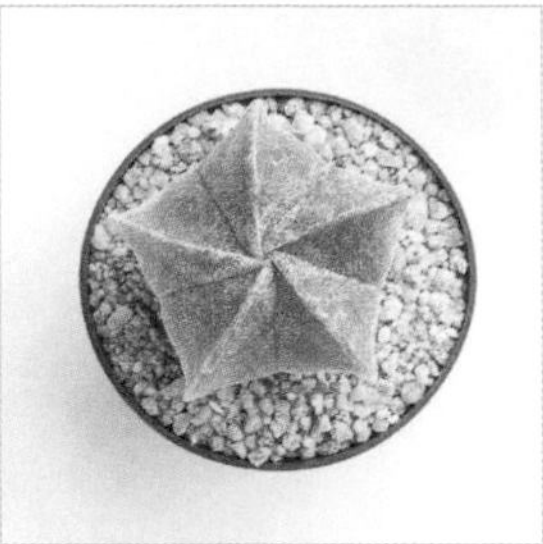
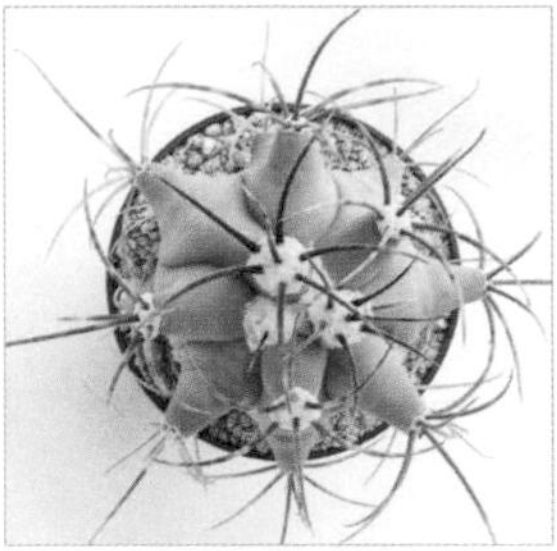
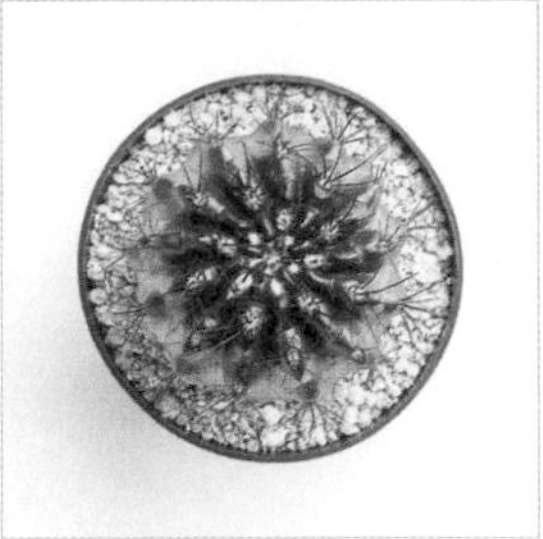
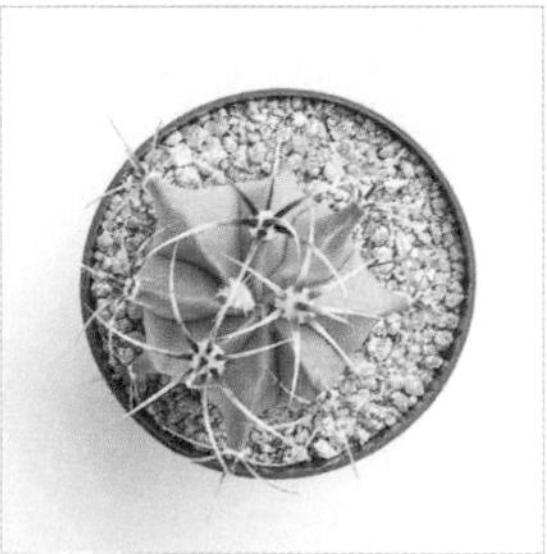
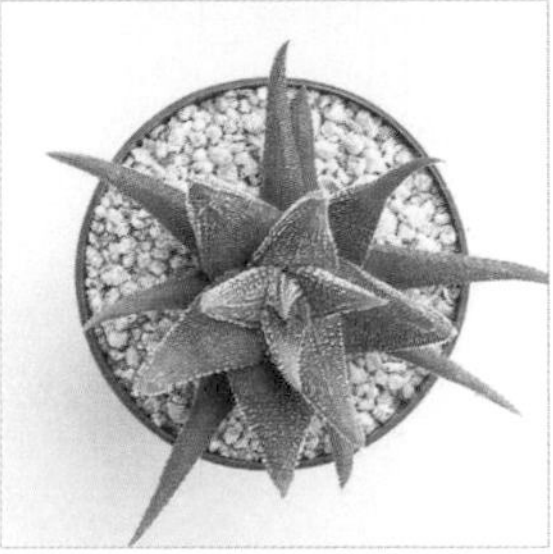
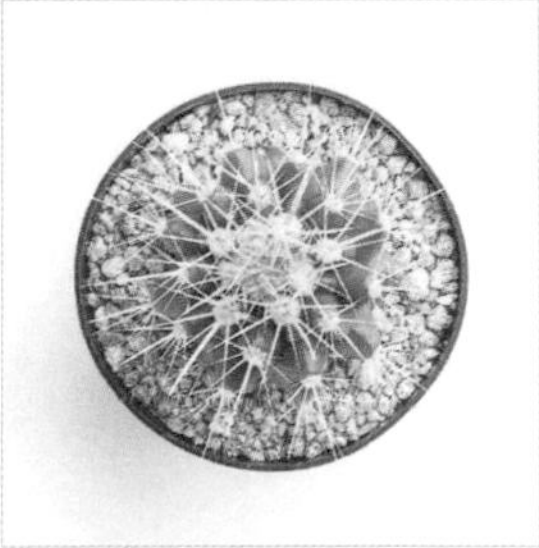
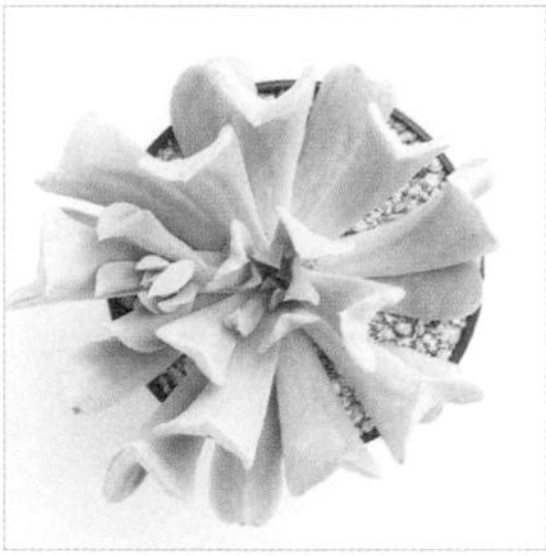
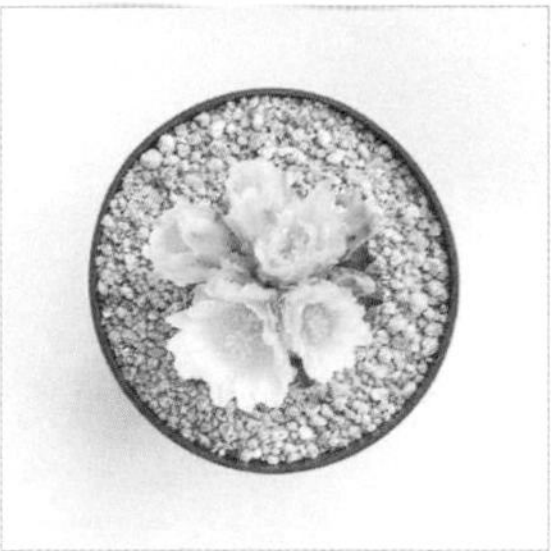
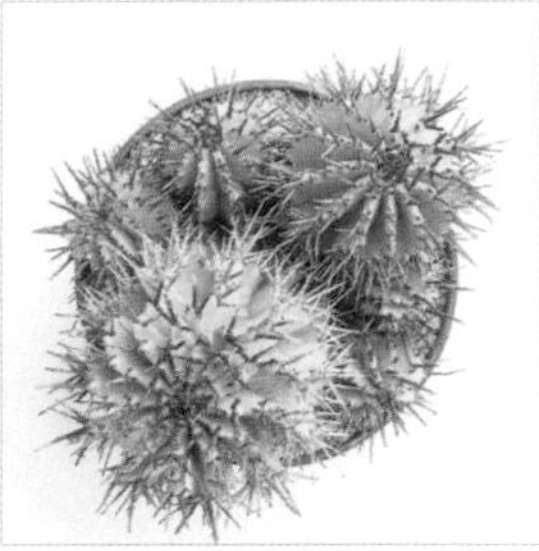
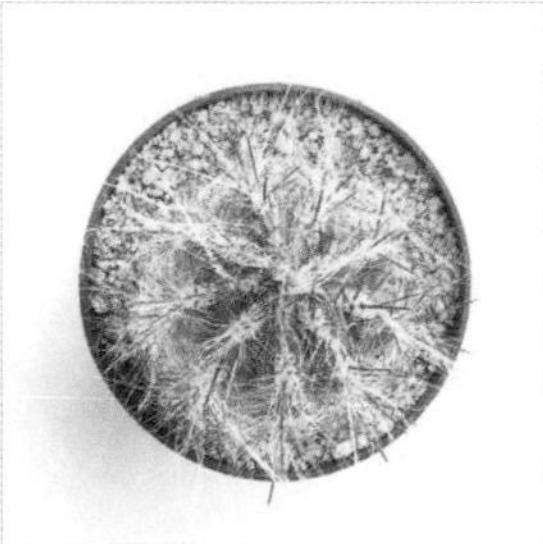
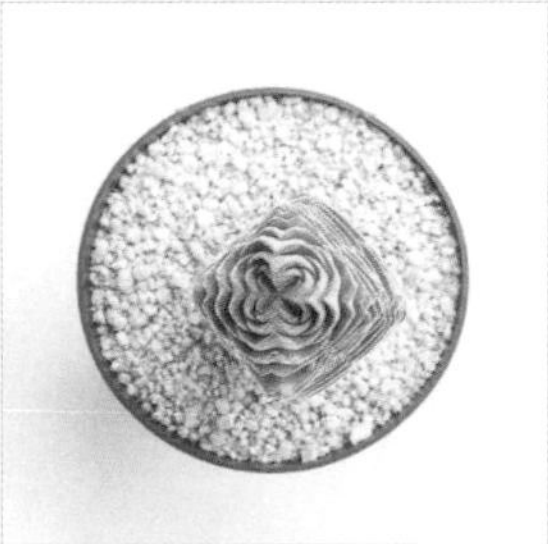
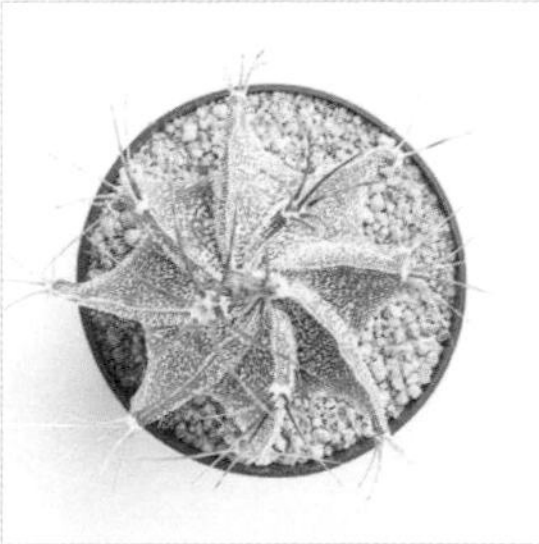
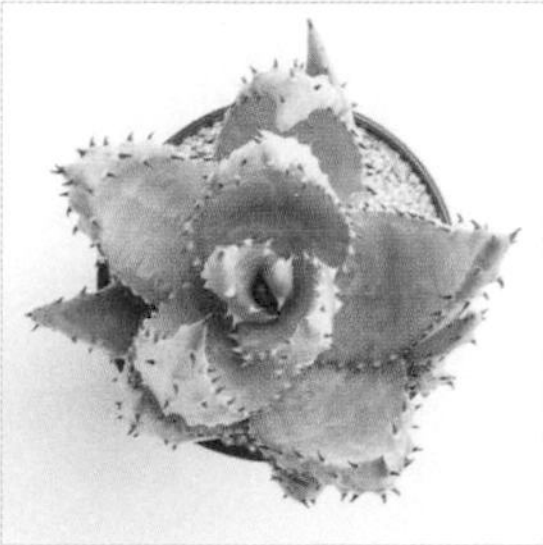
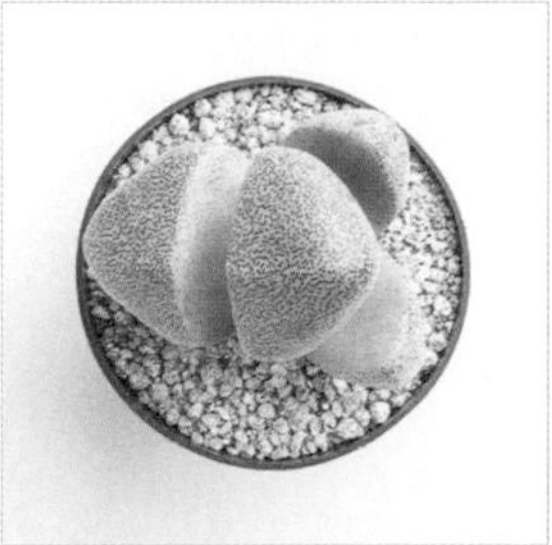
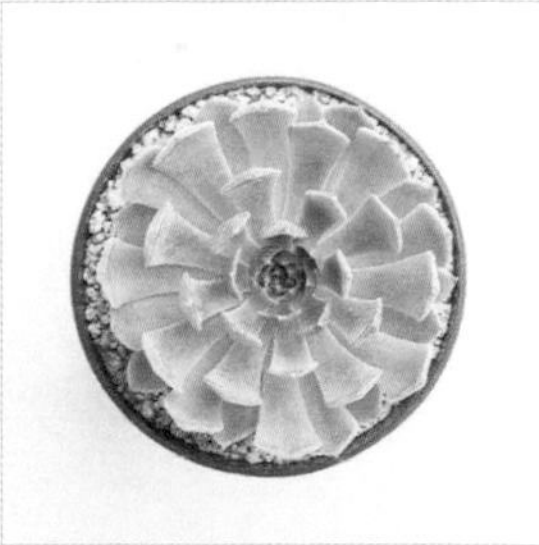

ADROMISCHUS COOPERI

ETYMOLOGY

The name *Adromischus* is derived from the Greek *hadros*, meaning "thick", and *mischos*, "stalk", while *cooperi* acknowledges Thomas Cooper, the 19th-century English botanist who collected it from South Africa.

PROFILE

This dwarf succulent grows to a maximum height of about 8cm (3in) and is characterized by camouflage-like markings on tubular leaves. Originating from South Africa and Namibia, it is an easy-going plant that grows in both summer and winter.

During the summer most have a tall 35-cm (14-in) flower stem adorned with small, bell-like, pink flowers. When thirsty, they will start to shed their leaves. Extremely hardy, they are able to survive to a minimum temperature of 3°C (37°F).

These plants are very easily propagated from individual leaves. In fact, this often happens naturally – if a leaf is knocked off or drops off naturally, and falls on the compost, it may sprout roots or a baby plant may appear. In this way you can create many plants from one (see pages 186–190).

AEONIUM ARBOREUM

ETYMOLOGY

The name *Aeonium* comes from the ancient Greek word *aionos*, for "ageless", while *arboreum* means "tree-like", from the Latin word for tree, *arbor*.

PROFILE

Native to the Canary Islands but also found in Madeira, Morocco and East Africa, this plant will reach a maximum height of 60cm (2ft), and is very hardy, down to a temperature of around 4°C (39°F).

It has unmissable dark purple/black rosettes, usually 10–25cm (4–10in) in diameter, which sit on a tall, smooth basal stem. Very bright sunlight is required to maintain the leaf colour. Large, pyramid-shaped clusters of bright yellow flowers appear in the spring.

Frequent problems include the leaves turning green, which means that the plant's not getting enough light, or the leaves shrivelling and falling in winter, which means that it's too dry.

AGAVE

ETYMOLOGY

The name *Agave* is derived originally from the Greek *agauē*, the feminine form of *agauós*, which means illustrious, noble and brilliant – very fitting for such a regal and magnificent genus of plant.

PROFILE

Agaves belong to the New World, populating Mexico, southwest United States, Central America and the West Indies. They are commonly mistaken for aloes (see page 37). Unlike aloes, agaves have fibres in their leaves and are monocarpic, meaning that they flower only once and then usually die.

These mainly stem-less plants have numerous large, long, rigid, fleshy leaves forming a rosette shape, usually with a very sharp tip. They are the most commonly grown and harvested succulent because of their many applications: the sap of some can be fermented to make pulque, which is distilled to produce the colourless spirit mescal; tequila is made from the sap of *Agave tequilana*; the nectar of some species has been used for centuries as a sweetener; and *Agave sisalana* is the source of the fibre sisal, for making rope and mats. The people of Mexico have used agaves in different ways for over 9,000 years.

AGAVE AMERICANA

ETYMOLOGY

This native of tropical America is most commonly known as American aloe or century plant, "century" referring to the long time it takes to flower. Once it does, the plant dies.

PROFILE

This plant is one of the most popular agaves, known best in its variegated forms: large, broad, rigid leaves with white or yellow margins or a central stripe. The leaves unfold from the centre of the rosette, often leaving an impression of the marginal spines on the underside of the younger leaves. Mature plants produce dense clusters of yellow flowers at the top of a long, tall, branched stem from spring to summer.

The size of these plants, up to 2m (6½ft) tall and 3m (10ft) wide, means that most are kept outside, but they should be brought indoors in the winter because they require protection from frost and snow.

AGAVE VICTORIAE-REGINAE

ETYMOLOGY

Named in 1875 by British horticulturist Thomas Moore in honour of Queen Victoria, this species of *Agave* has the common names of Queen Victoria agave and royal agave.

PROFILE

A native of the Chihuahuan Desert of Mexico, this is one of the slowest-growing agaves, characterized by dark green, polyhedral leaves, with a white outline and black tips, arranged in a compact rosette shape. The contrasts in colour and the plant's geometric form make it immensely sculptural and ornamental. Creamy white flowers are borne on spikes 2–4m (6½–13ft) high after 20–30 years.

Mature plants can reach 50cm (20in) in diameter, and survive temperatures as low as 10°C (50°F).

ALOE

ETYMOLOGY

Aloe is the Greek word for this succulent plant.

PROFILE

These succulents are native to South Africa, the Arabian Peninsula and Madagascar. There is astounding diversity within the genus, ranging from short grass aloes to humongous tree aloes, from smooth, fleshy leaves, usually with toothed edges, or leaves covered in bumps or short spines. Aloes are often confused with agaves, although, unlike agaves, they flower annually and are not as hardy – some agaves can tolerate temperatures below freezing.

Aloe is a genus containing over 500 species of flowering succulent plants. The most widely known is the fast-growing *Aloe vera*, or true aloe, which has been valued for hundreds of years for its medicinal properties and used topically as well as ingested.

ALOE ACULEATA

ETYMOLOGY

The species name *aculeata* is from the Latin word for "prickly". *Aloe aculeata* is also known by its common name of red-hot poker aloe.

PROFILE

Aloe aculeata is endemic to the Limpopo Valley and Mpumalanga in South Africa. It is a strikingly attractive plant, easily identified by its curved leaves that are the colour of a pink sunset and covered with small, warty growths. Spines are present only on the outside surface of the leaves, which are capable of reaching 30–60cm (1–2ft) in height.

Flowering occurs in mid- to late summer, and usually consists of a single cylindrical spike covered with orange-yellow, tubular flowers that hang downwards.

Due to habitat destruction and illegal harvesting, the numbers of this plant in the wild are declining and the species is listed as endangered.

ALOE VARIEGATA

ETYMOLOGY

The green and white stripes of this variegated aloe give it its common name of tiger aloe.

PROFILE

For me, this is the most attractive aloe. Originating from South Africa and eastern Africa, it is characterized by beautifully patterned and pointed dark green leaves, which are thick, triangular and indented on the inner side and make up rosettes that grow to 30cm (12in) in height. The plant becomes even more attractive in spring when it bears a spike adorned with salmon-pink flowers.

Aloe variegata is a great windowsill plant, as it enjoys having the maximum amount of light and the confines of a pot. It can survive temperatures as low as 7°C (45°F).

ASTROPHYTUM

ETYMOLOGY
The name of this genus is derived from the Greek word *aster*, meaning "star", and *phyton*, meaning "plant". Common names include bishop's hat, monk's hood and star cactus.

PROFILE
Native to the Chihuahuan Desert of Mexico, these cacti are usually solitary, cylindrical and star-shaped. There are four species in this genus – two that are spineless and two with prominent spines – ranging in height from 5–100cm (2in–3ft). Blooming over several weeks in the summer, they produce beautiful yellow flowers. On the following pages, I have described the two most common species of *Astrophytum*.

ASTROPHYTUM MYRIOSTIGMA

ETYMOLOGY
The species name is made up from the Greek words *myrios*, meaning "countless", and *stigma*, meaning "point".

PROFILE
This *Astrophytum* is characterized by a spineless, star-shaped body covered in white flecks, which are rough in texture. It reaches 10–25cm (4–10in) high and 10–18cm (4–7in) wide, and produces yellow flowers with red throats in summer. 'Nudum' is a smooth, green-bodied cultivar.

ASTROPHYTUM ORNATUM

ETYMOLOGY

The Latin word *ornare*, meaning "to decorate", is the root of this species name.

PROFILE

Astrophytum ornatum is dark green, 30–100cm (1–3ft) high, 15–30cm (6–12in) wide, with scattered white or yellow tuffs of hair-like growths called trichomes. Yellowish, wool-like areoles emit prominent spines, which begin as yellow but turn brown with age.

AUSTROCYLINDROPUNTIA

ETYMOLOGY

Two Latin words – *austro*, from *australis*, meaning "southern", and *cylindro*, from *cylindrus*, meaning "cylinder" – followed by the genus name *Opuntia* are the etymology for this genus.

PROFILE

These shrubby or tree-like cacti are, as the name suggests, closely related to *Opuntia* (see page 126). Their long, cylindrical stems are covered with bristles that, in mature plants, may irritate the skin and are difficult to remove, so display heavily spined mature plants out of harm's way.

AUSTROCYLINDROPUNTIA
CYLINDRICA

(SYN. OPUNTIA CYLINDRICA)

ETYMOLOGY

Giving this plant the species name *cylindrica* reinforces the impression of the cylindrical shape of its stems.

PROFILE

This plant, which is native to the highlands of Ecuador, is a shrubby or tree-like, branching cactus, with a mature height of around 4m (13ft). It is formed of dark green, cylindrical stems, with new stem segments sprouting laterally from existing ones. Red flowers appear from the apexes of stem segments, leaving shallow recesses once the flower has died.

The cristate, or crested, form of this plant, *Austrocylindropuntia cylindrica cristata* (syn. *Opuntia cylindrica cristata*) is characterized by its "fanned" stems of emerald green with white areoles and tiny spines.

AUSTROCYLINDROPUNTIA
VESTITA (SYN. OPUNTIA VESTITA)

ETYMOLOGY

The species name *vestita* refers to the plant's vestments, meaning its clothing of white hairs. Common names include cotton coral cactus, cotton pole and old man opuntia.

PROFILE

This native of the high altitudes of Bolivia forms slim cylindrical stems, 2–3cm (¾–1in) in diameter. They are covered with long, thin, white hairs, which give the plant a furry appearance and help to protect it from the sun. The stems can eventually grow to almost 60cm (2ft) tall.

Austrocylindropuntia vestita is a fickle bloomer, developing occasional deep red or violet flowers from the tops of the stems in spring and summer.

Austrocylindropuntia vestita 'Cristata' is the crested form of this plant and has unsegmented, undulating pads covered with fine white hairs.

BRASILIOPUNTIA BRASILIENSIS
(SYN. OPUNTIA BRASILIENSIS)

ETYMOLOGY

The name of this plant is derived from the words Brazil and *Opuntia* (see page 126). It goes by the common name of Brazilian prickly pear.

PROFILE

This cactus is found in Brazil, as you would expect, and also Paraguay, eastern Bolivia, Peru and northern Argentina.

It is the only species in the *Brasiliopuntia* genus. Its peculiar mode of growth makes it very easy to distinguish. It is one of the largest cacti, tree-like in stature – some grow up to 20m (65½ft) tall with trunks 35cm (14in) in diameter. It rises with a perfectly straight, cylindrical, slender-but-firm, woody trunk, which very gradually tapers to a point. The trunk is furnished with stem segments formed of bright green, flattened pads similar to most other *Opuntia* and giving the appearance of large leaves.

Its spines are thin, reddish or brownish, up to 15mm (½in) long and extremely sharp, so handle with caution. The pale yellow flowers open in spring to summer, appearing only on adult plants over 60–100cm (2–3ft) tall, and are followed by small, yellow fruits.

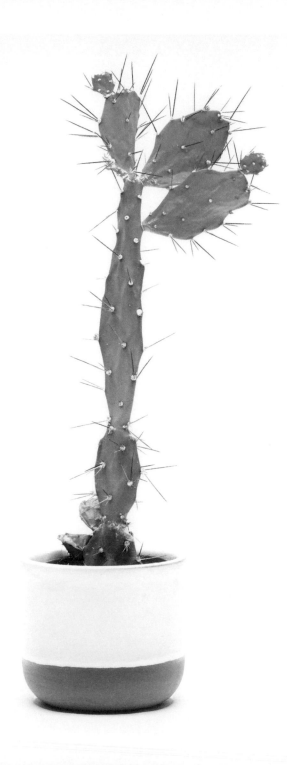

CEPHALOCEREUS SENILIS

ETYMOLOGY

The Greek for "head" (*kephale*) and the cactus genus *Cereus* (see page 50) are the roots of this genus name. *Senilis* comes from the Latin *senex*, meaning "old man" and refers to the plant's long white hairs.

Its common names include old man cactus, bunny cactus, old man of Mexico and white Persian cat cactus.

PROFILE

Native to Hidalgo and Guanajuato, Mexico, *Cephalocereus senilis* is a solitary, tall, columnar cactus, with a green stem that becomes grey over time and grows up to 15m (50ft) in height. The areoles produce long white hairs that eventually almost cover the grey spines.

CEREUS

ETYMOLOGY

Cereus in Latin means "waxy" or "candle", and refers to the candle-like form of the plants belonging to this genus, which was one of the first cactus genera to be established, in the mid-18th century.

PROFILE

The *Cereus* genus comprises 33 species of characteristically tall and columnar cacti. Fast-growing, they usually become too big for most people – although I personally don't believe in "too big" when it comes to cacti! Their large flowers, produced in summer only after 5–6 years, are variously pink, purple, cream, yellow or greenish. The flowers will only open at night, and will be closed again by the morning. People in some parts of the world will throw a party to wait up and see the flower open.

I've described my two favourite *Cereus* plants on the following pages. Their architectural qualities mean that they are wonderful to use indoors as statement pieces.

CEREUS REPANDUS 'FLORIDA'

ETYMOLOGY

The Latin *repandus*, meaning "bent backwards", gives us the English word "repand", which refers to the slightly uneven and wavy margins on the ribs of this cactus. *Florida* doesn't indicate the plant's geographical location, as you might think, but the plant's spectacular flowers – from the Latin *flos*, for "flower".

PROFILE

Native to the western Caribbean and Venezuela, this tall, tree-like cactus has tall, deep green stems that branch profusely. Its highly sculptural form makes it a very popular houseplant. Large, white, nocturnal flowers with reddish tips bloom from mature plants in late summer and early autumn.

CEREUS REPANDUS
F. MONSTROSA

ETYMOLOGY

The common names for this cactus include giant club cactus, hedge cactus and Peruvian apple cactus. The forma *monstrosa* typically indicates a strange or wonderful appearance.

PROFILE

This native of the western Caribbean and Venezuela has very distinctive stems: thick, firm with rounded ribs, an irregular texture and a branching habit. These qualities give the cactus an attractive sculptural form, making it a fantastic statement piece. White flowers bloom at night in early summer.

Growing like a tree, it can reach a height of up to 10m (33ft), often with many upright or slightly curved branches. Its common name of Peruvian apple cactus comes from the large, red, edible fruits that look much like an apple.

CLEISTOCACTUS

ETYMOLOGY

The genus name comes from the Greek *kleistos*, meaning "closed", because the flowers of these cacti hardly ever open.

PROFILE

These cylindrical cacti have fleshy stems with rounded ribs and many, many spines that can obscure the stems.

CLEISTOCACTUS MICROPETALUS

ETYMOLOGY

Micro and *petalus* allude to the small petals of the flowers of these cacti. Both words have Greek roots.

PROFILE

Native to Bolivia, *Cleistocactus micropetalus* is a columnar cactus with very slender green/grey stems bearing golden yellow spines. It is shrubby in form, branching at the base and spreading, reaching 1.5–3m (5–10ft) high. Green tubular flowers open at night in spring and early summer.

CLEISTOCACTUS STRAUSII

ETYMOLOGY

As its common name of silver torch cactus suggests, this tall plant has a silvery appearance.

PROFILE

Native to the mountainous areas of Peru, Uruguay, Bolivia and Argentina, *Cleistocactus strausii* is a tall columnar cacti growing to 1.5m (5ft). Its branched erect stems are densely covered with short white spines that give it a fluffy appearance. Once plants reach a height of around 50cm (20in), they can flower in the summer months, producing long, tubular, rose-red flowers scattered along the stems but, typically, they never open. In their natural habitat, these are pollinated by hummingbirds.

These cacti grow very quickly, so appreciate plenty of water and frequent doses of fertilizer.

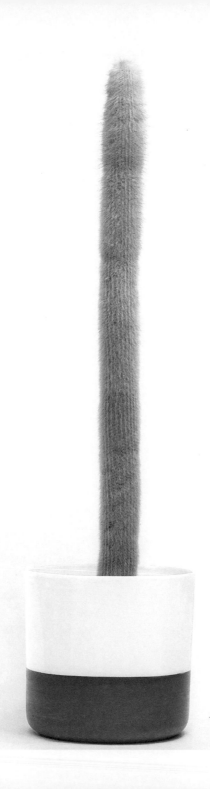

COCHEMIEA

ETYMOLOGY

This genus of cacti originates from the Baja Desert, in California, and is named after the Cochimí, a tribe of Native Americans that used to live there.

PROFILE

All species of *Cochemiea* feature short cylindrical stems that form small clumps of a dozen or more stems. In their native habitat, they prefer to grow in the cracks of rocks.

COCHEMIEA POSELGERI

ETYMOLOGY

The species name was given in honour of the 19th-century German botanist Dr Heinrich Poselger.

PROFILE

This was the first species of *Cochemiea* to be discovered and described, and is the best known. It has cylindrical stems, up to 2m (6½ft) high, covered in hooked spines. It blooms in late summer, when the tips of the stems are adorned with triumphant red, tubular flowers.

COPIAPOA

ETYMOLOGY

This genus is named after the town of Copiapó, located in northern Chile, which is surrounded by the Atacama Desert, from where the cactus originates.

PROFILE

These are globular or cylindrical cacti that range from tiny single heads to huge clumping masses consisting of hundreds of stems. In summer, all plants produce funnel-shaped, yellow flowers.

The spines may be long and fierce or, in contrast, almost completely absent. Coloration is also a variable, even within the same species, ranging from blue-green to deep green to brown.

The natural habitat of *Copiapoa* is very arid, which explains why their fibrous roots are sometimes larger than the plant above ground.

COPIAPOA TENUISSIMA

ETYMOLOGY

This species name comes from the Latin word *tenuis*, meaning "thin" or "slender", in reference to the small bodies and delicate spines of this cactus.

PROFILE

Usually up to 5cm (2in) in diameter, this cactus has a flattened to spherical shape and dull green/dark olive-green to almost purplish-black colouring. Well-defined ribs and a woolly apex give rise to yellow flowers in spring and summer. Single-headed or slowly clumping, but staying manageable in size, *Copiapoa* in cultivation will flower from a young age – and reliably, making it a popular plant for collectors.

COTYLEDON UNDULATA

ETYMOLOGY

In botany, Cotyledon is the name given to the first rudimentary leaves produced by a seedling. The word comes from the Greek, *kotulē*, meaning "cup-shaped". The Latin *unda*, meaning "wave", is the root of *undulata*. Silver crown and silver ruffles are among this plant's common names.

PROFILE

Cotyledon undulata is one of the most attractive and delicate succulents: a small shrub, characterized by blue/grey leaves covered in a chalky white coating, with wavy edges shaped like scallop shells. It originates from the Western Cape in South Africa and grows up to 50cm (20in) tall, with a flower stalk of 30–40cm (12–16in) long and orange-yellow blooms in autumn.

Try not to touch the leaves with your hands or get the leaves wet, otherwise you will remove the chalky bloom. In winter it requires a minimum temperature of 10°C (50°F).

CRASSULA

ETYMOLOGY

Crassula comes from the Latin *crassus*, meaning "thick", referring to the succulent leaves.

PROFILE

Over 300 species of *Crassula* exist, mostly originating from South Africa's Western Cape and Eastern Cape provinces. This genus contains one of the most common succulent houseplants, *Crassula ovata* (see page 66).

The different species are determined by their flower shape. Many are characterized by exquisite geometric forms, usually made up of pairs of leaves stacked on top of each other at 90-degree angles. Most *Crassula* remain small. They enjoy moderate watering all year round, except just after flowering.

Crassula are highly susceptible to fungi and pests.

CRASSULA ARBORESCENS SUBSP. UNDULATIFOLIA

ETYMOLOGY

Commonly called ripple jade, this plant's species name, *arborescens*, comes from the Latin for "becoming more tree-like", from *arbor*, meaning "tree". The Latin *unda*, for "wave", *latus*, for "broad", and *folium*, for "leaf", is the etymology of *undulatifolia*.

PROFILE

Native to the Eastern Cape, South Africa, these plants are characterized by their tongue-shaped, grey-to-blue-green, twisted leaves, edged in purple. The colour reflects the sun and helps the plant to stay cool during very hot days. In spring right through to summer clusters of white and pink star-shaped flowers may completely cover the plant.

It forms a large branched, bonsai-like tree, 60cm–2m (2–6½ft) tall, similar to the jade plant, *Crassula ovata* (see page 66).

CRASSULA 'BUDDHA'S TEMPLE'

ETYMOLOGY

This is not a naturally occurring plant but a hybrid, introduced in 1959 by the American horticulturist Myron Kimnach, who cross-pollinated *Crassula pyramidalis* and *C. perfoliata* var. *falcata*.

PROFILE

What makes this plant so fascinating is its perfectly geometrical, almost architectural, form.

The leaves are greyish-green, scale-like, turned up at the ends and arranged in a tight, square, columnar rosette, approximately 4cm (1½in) wide. They grow to approximately 15cm (6in) in height. The light, white, powdery surface helps to preserve moisture and protect from strong sunlight.

Bright red buds open to reveal small pink, almost white, flowers, densely clustered at the tip of the plant, in summer.

CRASSULA OVATA

ETYMOLOGY

The species name *ovata* is from the Latin for "egg-shaped".
Its common names are jade plant, friendship tree, lucky plant
and money tree.

PROFILE

Native to South Africa and Mozambique, *Crassula ovata* is a
succulent characterized by shiny, jade-green, spoon-shaped
leaves, sometimes with red edges. Mature plants bloom in the
summer, producing delicate pink or white, star-shaped flowers.

A very common houseplant worldwide, it can reach a maximum
height of 1.5m (5ft). It likes a sunny position with a minimum
temperature of 4°C (39°F).

CYLINDROPUNTIA SPINOSIOR
(SYN. OPUNTIA SPINOSIOR)

ETYMOLOGY

Named from the Latin *spinosus*, meaning "spiny", for the number of spines per areole, this cactus is commonly known as cane cholla, spiny cholla and walkingstick cactus.

PROFILE

This plant is a native of Arizona and New Mexico, and also Sonora and Chihuahua in Mexico, and makes a compact, tree-like cactus, with bright green stems and whorled branches covered in spines. It can grow up to 2m (6½ft) tall. Large, bright pink, purple, white or yellow flowers cover the plant in spring.

ECHEVERIA

ETYMOLOGY

The Mexican botanical artist Atanasio Echeverría provides the name behind this genus. He made the first drawings of these succulents in the late 18th century,

PROFILE

These plants are native to the mountainous terrains of Mexico, Argentina and Texas. There are over 150 different types, each characterized by thick fleshy leaves in a rosette shape (see opposite for one of my favourite varieties). These rosettes vary from a compact solitary form to clumps with multiple smaller rosettes at the base. There is such a beautiful range of colours and textures, from greyish blue to pink, green, red and black. Some have a chalky white coating, while others are shiny and waxy; some have ruffled edges, others, pointy.

Sunlight is needed to ensure the beautiful leaf colour and overall healthy appearance of *Echeveria*, so avoid shady locations. Having said that, if the temperature is over 30°C (86°F), you will need to provide shade and extra ventilation.

I find it easier to water these plants from underneath, as stagnant water pooling on the leaves can damage them.

Many *Echeveria* can become leggy, forming a long stem and eventually toppling over. To prevent this, you can de-head the plant by cutting the neck about 3cm (1in) below the lowest leaves with a sharp knife. Leave the cut-off head for a few weeks until it forms roots, plant in new compost and wait for new rosettes to develop. The cut stem will also develop new rosettes. Plants all round!

ECHEVERIA ELEGANS

ETYMOLOGY

As you might guess, *elegans* means "elegant", from the Latin. Mexican snowball and white Mexican rose are the common names of this species.

PROFILE

Echeveria elegans is the most popular variety of *Echeveria*. – and one of my favourites. A blue/grey, fleshy succulent with leaves arranged in tight rosettes, it grows to 5–10cm (2–4in) tall, with long, slender, pink stalks of pink flowers with yellow tips in winter and spring.

It will not tolerate temperatures below 7°C (45°F).

ECHINOCACTUS

ETYMOLOGY

The genus takes its name from the Greek words *echinos*, meaning "hedgehog", and *kaktos*, meaning "thistle".

PROFILE

Natives of Mexico and southwest United States, these slow-growing cacti can be spherical, columnar or shaped like barrels. Their prominent ribs are densely covered in spines.

ECHINOCACTUS GRANDIS

ETYMOLOGY

As the species name suggests, this plant is also known as large barrel cactus or giant barrel cactus. It is also identified by the name *Echinocactus platyacanthas*.

PROFILE

Originating from northern and central Mexico, the young *Echinocactus grandis* is characterized by a dusty green, globular body with obtuse ribs, and long, very flamboyant, sometimes curved spines with yellow/white, felt-like areoles. This solitary cactus grows oblong with age, reaching a maximum height of 3m (10ft) and 1m (3ft) in diameter, with the mature version looking very different from the young.

Vivid yellow flowers are produced at the end of spring or in early summer.

ECHINOCACTUS GRUSONII

ETYMOLOGY

This species of cactus was named for Hermann Gruson, a 19th-century German plant collector. Its common names include golden barrel cactus and mother-in-law's seat.

PROFILE

Originating from the Rio Moctezuma Valley in Querétaro, Central Mexico, this solitary, globular cactus becomes elongated with age to form a barrel shape up to 50cm (20in) in height. It is characterized by deep ridges with fierce yellow spines. Yellow flowers, up to 6cm (2½in) in height, are produced in summer, but only on mature plants.

In their natural habitat, these cacti tend to lean to the south or southwest so that the spines can better protect the body of the plant from the harsh desert sun. In fact, desert travellers can use the plant as a compass.

The species is currently listed as endangered in the wild after the creation of dams – specifically the Zimapán Dam and Reservoir in Mexico – in the 1990s.

ECHINOCEREUS

ETYMOLOGY

This cactus genus takes its name from the Greek word *echinos*, meaning "hedgehog", and the genus *Cereus* (see page 50), implying "spiny Cereus".

PROFILE

These very popular cacti have some of the most brilliantly coloured flowers in the cactus family, ranging from a sizzling pink to bright yellow. They're also small plants, making them particularly suited to indoor growing.

ECHINOCEREUS BRANDEGEEI

ETYMOLOGY

The early 20th-century American botanist Katharine Brandegee is the name behind this species. Its common names include strawberry cactus and strawberry hedgehog.

PROFILE

Endemic to the Baja California region, this fierce-looking cactus is covered in sharp, dagger-like spines. The stems always grow in clusters, which vary from a few stems to great clumps more than 2m (6½ft) across and 35cm (14in) tall. Purple, funnel-shaped flowers appear on the plant's stems in summer.

This desert plant tolerates full exposure to sunlight. It tends to bronze in strong light, which encourages spine production. For short periods, it is frost-hardy to -5°C (23°F).

ECHINOCEREUS RIGIDISSIMUS

ETYMOLOGY

The species name comes from the Latin *rigidus*, meaning "rigid" or "stiff", referencing the plant's spines. It is commonly named Arizona rainbow or hedgehog cactus.

PROFILE

This native of Chihuahua and Sonora in Mexico, and also Arizona and New Mexico, grows mainly at high altitudes or on gravelly hills and steep canyon sides.

It is a truly beautiful cactus that rarely branches or produces offsets with age, remaining a solitary, short, cylindrical cactus 6–20cm (2½–8in) tall. The fine, rigid radial spines are either straight or slightly curved towards the stem. Its common name of Arizona rainbow is derived from the alternating coloured bands of spines of grey, reddish brown, bright pink or pink and white that differentiate each year's growth.

Good light exposure is needed to maintain the beautiful colour of this plant. It blooms from late spring to summer with bright pink flowers up to 10cm (4in) in diameter.

Echinocereus rigidissimus is very sensitive to overwatering and is hardy to temperatures of -12°C (10°F).

ECHINOPSIS

ETYMOLOGY

Named from the Greek *echinos*, meaning "hedgehog" or "sea urchin", and *opsis*, meaning "appearance".

PROFILE

Cacti in this genus are shrubby or tree-like, and produce very showy flowers in a wide range of colours from spring to summer, although they rarely last more than a day.

ECHINOPSIS ATACAMENSIS SUBSP. PASACANA
(SYN. TRICHOCEREUS PASACANA)

ETYMOLOGY

The species name references the Atacama Desert in South America. The fruit that these cacti produce goes by the vernacular name of *pasacana*.

PROFILE

Found mostly on steep slopes in its native Argentina and Bolivia, this columnar cactus often forms branches and grows to 10m (33ft) high. Its wood is hardy and used in construction, as well as for making rain sticks (a kind of musical instrument that mimics the sound of rain falling). From spring to summer white flowers with a red tint grow laterally from the stem.

ECHINOPSIS SUBDENUDATA

ETYMOLOGY

The species name is from the Latin *sub*, meaning "almost", and *denudatus*, meaning "worn off", in reference to the plant's short spines. It is more commonly known as Easter lily cactus or night-blooming hedgehog.

PROFILE

Originating in the Entre Ríos Province of Bolivia, and possibly Paraguay, this cactus is very minimal in form. It has a depressed, dark green stem with subtle ribs.

The woolly cream areoles are dotted around the plant with perfect symmetry, like polka dots. From them arise the spines, but they are so tiny that they are almost hidden by the areoles.

These plants need full exposure to light, with full sun or half-shade in summer. From late spring to the end of summer, they produce large, stunning, white to light pink, funnel-shaped, fragrant flowers. Night-blooming, the flowers usually last for just 24 hours.

EPIPHYLLUM ANGULIGER

ETYMOLOGY

Epiphyllum is Greek for "upon the leaf", and *anguliger* means "angle bearing", denoting the deeply toothed stems of this plant.

Common names include fishbone cactus, zigzag cactus, moon cactus and queen of the night.

PROFILE

The species, native to Mexico, is a hanging plant, often grown as an ornamental for its long, wide, toothed, bright green stems and beautiful, fragrant flowers in autumn. It also produces a gooseberry-like fruit.

Like all epiphytes, *Epiphyllum anguliger* prefers shade, with a few hours of sunshine.

ERIOSYCE TALTALENSIS SUBSP. PAUCICOSTATA

ETYMOLOGY

The Greek words *erion*, meaning "wool", and *syke*, "fig tree", referencing the wool-covered fruit, are behind this genus name. The species name, *taltalensis*, comes from the city of Taltal in Antofagasta, Chile, while the subspecies is made up of the Latin words *paucus*, for "few", and *costa*, for "rib".

PROFILE

Native to the coast and coastal hills of the province of Antofagasta, Chile, this grey-blue-green, often grey-purple-tinged, solitary, globular cactus elongates with age to a columnar shape, 15–30cm (6–12in) in height, with only 8–12 very pronounced ribs and dark brown to black spines, soon becoming greyish. It starts flowering when young, producing very pale pink, cream-white or pale yellowish, scentless flowers from mid-spring through to late summer.

The plants obtain most of their water from condensation in the air, and are hardy down to a minimum temperature of -5°C (23°F).

ESPOSTOA

ETYMOLOGY

This genus of cacti is named after the renowned early 20th-century Peruvian botanist Nicolas E. Esposto.

PROFILE

Originating from the Andes of southern Ecuador and northern Peru, this genus of white columnar cacti is appreciated for its decorative qualities, in particular for its white fleece. This is often perceived as soft and fluffy but actually consists of many sharp central spines.

ESPOSTOA NANA
(SYN. PSEUDOESPOSTOA NANA, ESPOSTOA MELANOSTELE SUBSP. NANA)

ETYMOLOGY

Nana comes from the Latin word nanus, meaning "small" or "dwarf". The common names for this species include Peruvian Old Lady and Dwarf Old Man cacti.

PROFILE

This columnar cactus is characterized by the long white hairs that densely cover the whole stem to make it look far from your average cactus. A shrub-like cactus, *Epostoa Nana* originates from Peru and grows to a maximum height of 1.5m (5ft).

White, bell-shaped flowers, which open at night, are produced from late spring to early summer. The plant also bears tiny, bright green, sweet fruit in summer.

EUPHORBIA

ETYMOLOGY

This genus was named in honour of Euphorbus, a 1st-century AD
Greek physician, who discovered the first succulent species in
the Atlas Mountains. He was physician to King Juba of
Mauretania, an ancient region of North Africa.

PROFILE

Euphorbias originate from the Old World (the part of the
world known to Europeans before the discovery of the
Americas) and are found specifically in subtropical regions
of Africa, Arabia and Thailand.

The genus comprises over 2,000 species, with almost 500
of them being succulents – some of my favourites feature
on the following pages. They are one of the most popular
succulent plants because of their incredible range of size,
form and structure. Many beautiful and intriguing hybrids
exist and continue to be created yearly.

A white milky sap called latex is common to all of them.
It is poisonous when ingested and irritating to the skin and,
especially, the eyes. If you get any on your hands, wash them
immediately with soap and water.

EUPHORBIA AMMAK VARIEGATA

ETYMOLOGY

Ammak is the vernacular Arabic name for *Euphorbia ammak variegata*, while *variegata* indicates that this plant has variegated leaves. Its common names include variegated African candelabra and ghost euphorbia.

PROFILE

Originating from Yemen and Saudi Arabia, this sturdy, columnar succulent has thick, wavy-edged leaves covered with short dark spines. Reaching a maximum height of 3–4m (10–13ft), it can branch off when truncated.

It is a truly beautiful plant that enhances any plant collection with its strong, sculptural quality twinned with its overall very pale green/cream-white appearance. Placed among the green of most houseplants, it creates wonderful contrast and variation.

EUPHORBIA CANARIENSIS

ETYMOLOGY

A native of the Canary Islands, hence its species name, this succulent is commonly called Canary Island spurge, Canary candelabra spurge or Hercules club.

PROFILE

Euphorbia canariensis occurs in lava formations on the barren shores and south-facing mountain slopes of all the Canary Islands. It is one of the most abundant plants on the sea cliffs.

A fleshy, columnar succulent, it grows up to 4m (13ft) high, with quadrangular or pentagonal trunks. It is cactus-like in form, clumping from the base, with one trunk producing more than 150 branches. The stems are furnished with pairs of dark, cow-horn-shaped spines.

These plants come in two different stem colours: a lime-green form, *E. canariensis* f. *viridis* (also known as "green type" or "green form"), and a darker green, known as *E. canariensis*.

Dark red to reddish-green flowers appear on the tops of the stem ridges from late spring to early summer.

EUPHORBIA CANDELABRUM
(SYN. EUPHORBIA ERITREA, E. ACRURENSIS)

ETYMOLOGY

Candelabrum is Latin for "candlestick", referring to this plant's structure of branching stems. Its common names are candelabra tree and milk tree.

PROFILE

This is one of the most popular succulents for the home, where it grows very happily. Often mistaken for a cactus, it provides the cactus-like form but at a much faster rate, quickly reaching ceiling height. It forms a dense crown of ascending branches and both the main stem and the multiple dividing branches usually consist of 3–5 ribs that can be wavy and twisted, with thin walls and sparse triangular spines along their edges.

Rounded heads of small, yellow-green flowers appear on the the tips of the plant's ridges in spring.

When moved the plant's columns can sometimes collide with each other, causing permanent scarring, so it is best to place it in a location where there are no chances of collision and, when moving it, try placing wrapping between the branches.

Originating from Eritrea, South Africa and Eastern Africa, this succulent shares characteristics with other *Euphorbia* species, such as *E. abyssinica* var. *erythraeae* and *E. ingens*, which often makes precise identification difficult.

EUPHORBIA 'COCKLEBUR'
(SYN. EUPHORBIA × JAPONICA)

ETYMOLOGY

For very obvious reasons when you look at it, this succulent is commonly known as a pineapple plant.

PROFILE

One of the most popular *Euphorbia* hybrids, this intriguing plant is a cross between *E. susannae* and *E. bupleurifolia*. It resembles a multi-headed pineapple, with each head growing to a maximum diameter of 4cm (1½in). This plant does not bear flowers.

The stems are fat and globular with a diamond pattern, brown/green and woody in appearance, and covered with 1-cm (½-in) long, green leaves.

EUPHORBIA ENOPLA

ETYMOLOGY

This species is named from the Greek *enoplos*, meaning "armed", referring to the thick spines. Its common name is, appropriately, the pincushion euphorbia.

PROFILE

A native of South Africa, *Euphorbia enopla* is a grey-green succulent with heavily branching, finger-sized stems. These grow to about 30–100cm (1–3ft) and are densely covered with thick, long red spines. It is a very attractive and popular plant.

Tiny, dark red flowers form on the tips of the spines in summer.

EUPHORBIA FLANAGANII

ETYMOLOGY

The species name is courtesy of Henry Flanagan, the 19th-century South African plant collector. The plant is commonly known as green coral or Medusa's head, because of its snake-like "arms".

PROFILE

Native to the Eastern Cape, South Africa, *Euphorbia flanaganii* is a low, spineless, multi-branched succulent. It grows to 5cm (2in) tall and 30cm (12in) wide. This plant does not bear flowers.

Euphorbia flanaganii f. *cristata* is the crested form. There are two types: one with a crested central shoot, along with normal cylindrical lateral shoots, and one with crested lateral shoots only. Crested forms of the plant grown in full sun often take on a bronze coloration, especially in winter.

EUPHORBIA HORRIDA

ETYMOLOGY

The Latin word *horridus* is the root of the species name. Meaning "bristly", "prickly" or "rough", it refers to the plant's numerous strong spines. Its common name is the African milk barrel.

PROFILE

Native to the Western Cape of South Africa, *Euphorbia horrida* has erect cylindrical stems up to 15cm (6in) thick and 1–1.5m (3–5ft) tall, with 6–20 ribs.

The spines are actually the dried remnants of its flower stalks and differ in form, size and hardiness, although they are usually rather thick and a dark purple/grey colour.

Very small flowers, ranging from yellowish-green to dark purple, appear in spring and summer.

There are several varieties of this succulent; one of my favourites is the dwarf whitish form *Euphorbia horrida* 'Snowflake'.

EUPHORBIA LACTEA

ETYMOLOGY

The whitish markings on the branches of *Euphorbia lactea* provide the species name, from the Latin for "milk-white". The plant is commonly known as mottled spurge, dragon bones, milk stripe euphorbia, candelabra cactus or candelabrum tree, due to its highly branching characteristic and the light green mid-stripe that appears on the branches.

PROFILE

Native to tropical Asia, this plant grows into a tall shrub, reaching a height of 5m (16ft) at maturity. It is dark green in colour with branches displaying a central stripe of greenish white. The spines are in very short pairs, about 2–5mm (⅛–¼in) in length, and the leaves are just as minute. Hardy to 5°C (41°F), these plants grow very well in pots and, as they originate from subtropical climates, they flourish in humid environments.

When grown at home, these plants rarely flower.

EUPHORBIA LACTEA 'CRISTATA'

ETYMOLOGY

The crested form of the species; this plant is more commonly known as the crested elkhorn, crested candelabra plant, crested euphorbia or spring horse.

PROFILE

A beautiful and intriguing plant, its elaborate, fan-shaped branches form in a cluster or wavy shape. Commonly found in dark green and attractively marked with silver-grey zigzag patterns, the plant is also available in a variety of variegated species, ranging in colour from white to yellow, pink, violet and green. These are commonly seen as grafts (as shown here), with *E. lactea* grafted on top of *E. neriifolia*, commonly but incorrectly referred to as coral cactus.

When grown at home, these plants rarely flower.

EUPHORBIA OBESA

ETYMOLOGY

The species name is from the Latin for "fat", but this succulent is more commonly known as the basketball plant.

PROFILE

Small but plump-looking, this subtropical succulent is native to South Africa. It is characterized by its green/grey-striped, spineless, chunky, globose stem, with eight radial ribs making perfect circle segments, just like an orange. Reaching a maximum diameter of 10cm (4in), it is initially ball-shaped but can become elongated with age.

Tiny, yellow-green flowers cluster on the apex of *Euphorbia obesa* in summer.

EUPHORBIA TRIGONA F. RUBRA

ETYMOLOGY

The name is derived from the Latin *triangulus*, for "triangular", relating to the three rib triangular shape of the stems. *Rubra* indicates that it is the red form. It is commonly known as the African milk tree.

PROFILE

This columnar succulent has branches growing from the base, covered with long-lasting, blade-shaped leaves. Both the stems and leaves are flushed a purplish-red. Growing up to 3m (10ft) in height, the plant is popular with collectors and the design-conscious who wish to add vibrant and unique colours to their interior landscape.

This plant does not bear flowers.

FAUCARIA TIGRINA

ETYMOLOGY

This plant's name comes from the Latin words *fauces*, meaning "throat", and *tigrinus*, meaning "tiger-like", referencing the strongly toothed leaves that resemble a tiger's jaws. It is commonly known as tiger jaws or shark's jaws.

PROFILE

Native to South Africa's Eastern Province and the Karoo desert, *Faucaria tigrina* is a small plant, measuring 8cm (3in) in diameter, with thick, triangular leaves. The plants are light green, turning purple if exposed to strong sunshine. The leaf edges are lined with long, whisker-like teeth in opposite pairs. These threadlike structures are special adaptations that help to collect water vapour from the surrounding air and direct it down towards the roots of the plant.

In summer, golden yellow flowers appear in the centre of the rosette of leaves.

FEROCACTUS

ETYMOLOGY

The genus name is made up from the Latin *ferox*, meaning
"brave", "armed" or "wild", and *cactus*.

PROFILE

This genus hails from the southwestern United States and
Mexico. Most are barrel-shaped, and all of them have stout
spines, the colours of which vary, from white through yellow
to red. Their flowers, which can be yellow to red, form in
clusters at the top of the plant.

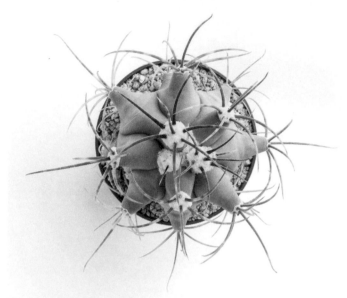

FEROCACTUS EMORYI

ETYMOLOGY

The species name is in honour of Major William H. Emory, the 19th-century American officer who was in charge of the United States-Mexican boundary survey of 1848–53. The plant's common names are Emory's barrel cactus, Coville's barrel cactus and traveller's friend.

PROFILE

Native to the lower deserts of Arizona and Mexico, this beautiful member of the *Ferocactus* genus is very popular in cultivation because it blooms early, from mid-summer to early autumn. It is a tall, solitary, barrel cactus with colourful, usually red, spines, growing to a mature height of 2m (6½ft) and over 80cm (2½ft) wide. Its red flowers are followed by yellow, oblong fruit.

FEROCACTUS LATISPINUS

ETYMOLOGY

The name of this species is derived from the Latin *latus*, meaning
"broad", and *spinus*, meaning "spine". It is, however, more commonly
known as devil's tongue barrel, crow's claw cactus or candy cactus.

PROFILE

Native to Mexico, *Ferocactus latispinus* grows as a single, light
green, globular cactus, reaching 30cm (12in) in height and 40cm
(16in) across. Its spines range from reddish to white in colour,
with the central spine flat, wide and hooked, giving the plant
a "gnarly" look.

It blooms in late autumn to early winter, producing "glassy",
violet or yellow flowers, up to 6cm (2in) long and 3cm (1in) wide.

FRITHIA PULCHRA

ETYMOLOGY

The genus *Frithia* is named after English-born Frank Frith (1872–1954), a horticulturist, who settled in South Africa and took specimens of the genus to Kew Gardens during a visit to London. The species name is derived from the Latin *pulcher*, meaning "beautiful". The plant's common names include baby toes and fairy elephant's feet.

PROFILE

Native to South Africa, this low-growing succulent has erect, club-shaped leaves with clear, almost granular leaf tips, sprouting purple, daisy-like flowers in summer.

Frithia is a summer grower and will take as much light as you can give it, but fierce direct sunshine could cause scorching. During periods of drought, it shrinks in size as a result of moisture loss. Plants may even disappear below the grit under extreme conditions.

GASTERIA CARINATA
VAR. VERRUCOSA
(SYN. GASTERIA VERRUCOSA)

ETYMOLOGY

Gasteria derives from the Greek *gaster*, meaning "stomach", relating to the similarity in shape of the flowers to a stomach. *Carinata* means "keel-shaped", from the Latin *carina*, for "keel", while *verrucosa* is Latin for "rough" or "warty".

The common names are easier to digest, and include tongue aloe, sago plant, warted aloe, warty aloe, ox tongue and deer's tongue.

PROFILE

This succulent is mostly green, with smooth leaves covered in white tubercles. It is unusual in shape and form, with thick leaves growing laterally and younger ones forming perpendicular to them, creating an attractive clump 3–18cm (1–7in) tall and 15–80cm (6in–2½ft) wide. Many very beautiful variegated hybrids exist. The plants prefer half-shade.

The *Gasteria* genus is closely related to the *Aloe*.

GYMNOCALYCIUM

ETYMOLOGY

Gymnocalycium is derived from the Greek *gymnos*, meaning
"naked", and *kalyx*, meaning "bud", referring to the flower buds that
bear no hair or spines. It is commonly known as the chin cactus.

PROFILE

Native to Argentina, southern Bolivia and parts of Uruguay,
Paraguay and Brazil, most species are rather small (4–15cm/
1½–6in high), globose, solitary plants with ribs that are often only
somewhat tuberculate. This slight punctuation along the ribs
results in a chin-like appearance, hence its common name.

In cultivation *Gymnocalycium* are popular for their easy
flowering habits – the flowers are generally a brightly coloured
yellow, pink, orange or red. In all species, the petals are
smooth and the flowers need high temperatures (around
25°C/77°F) in order to open.

GYMNOCALYCIUM MIHANOVICHII VAR. FRIEDRICHII 'RUBRA'

ETYMOLOGY

The 20th-century Yugoslavian shipping magnate and patron of botany Nicolas Mihanovich is the name behind the species, while the variety is in honour of the 20th-century German cactus collector Adolfo Friedrich. 'Rubra' means "red". The plant's common name is lollipop cactus, reflecting the vivid colour of the flowers.

PROFILE

This unusually coloured cactus is one of the most popular *Gymnocalycium*. It is a bright red mutation of the normally grey-green or reddish-green species. Lacking chlorophyll, it cannot photosynthesize, which means that it needs to be grafted onto another cactus with chlorophyll, usually a *Hylocereus*, to stay alive.

The plant can reach a height of more than 10cm (4in) and a spread of 6–12cm (2¼–5in), often branching profusely from the sides. It bears pale pink-purple flowers.

HAWORTHIA

ETYMOLOGY
Named for Adrian H. Haworth (1768–1833), English zoologist, botantist and succulent plant specialist.

PROFILE
Native to South Africa, these succulents are ideal for growing in pots due to their small size and durability. Their appearance resembles that of small aloes, except for the characteristic small white flowers shared throughout the genus. Most species are stemless with dark, firm leaves, but others have soft leaves with transparent 'leaf windows'.

HAWORTHIA EMELYAE

ETYMOLOGY
This species of *Haworthia* is named for Emily Ferguson, a 20th-century South African plant collector.

PROFILE
Growing to a maximum height of about 40cm (16in), this succulent is characterized by bulbous, "juicy-looking" succulent leaves arranged in a rosette shape that reaches up to 10cm (4in) across. The leaves, which are decorated with vein line striations, turn a very attractive sunset pink when exposed to the sun. A stem grows from the middle of the plant in early spring, bearing tubular white flowers.

HAWORTHIA REINWARDTII

ETYMOLOGY

The species owes its name to Caspar Reinwardt, a 19th-century Dutch botanist.

PROFILE

This plant is native to the Eastern Cape province of South Africa, and is one of the species of *Haworthia* commonly cultivated as an ornamental.

Numerous, densely arranged, rigid, dark green leaves create columnar stems growing to 20–35cm (8–14in) in height, with a rosette of overlapping, white-spotted, fleshy leaves arranged in a spiral pattern. Racemes of tubular white/pink flowers appear in spring.

A winter grower, it is dormant in the hottest summer months. It needs light to moderate shade, but will take full sun for part of the day – sunshine is needed to preserve the coloration of the leaves. It is hardy to temperatures as low as -5°C (23°F).

HOYA KERRII

ETYMOLOGY

Hoya is named for Thomas Hoy (c.1750–1821), the English head gardener at the Duke of Northumberland's Syon House in Middlesex, England. The species name is attributed to the Irish physician and botanist Arthur Francis George Kerr, who first collected this succulent in Thailand.

Common names include wax hearts, sweetheart hoya, sweetheart plant, valentine hoya, porcelain flower, heart leaf and lucky hearts.

PROFILE

As well as Thailand, the plant is also a native of south China, Vietnam, Laos, Cambodia and the Indonesian island of Java.

Hoya kerrii is a robust climbing plant that can grow up to 4m (13ft) high. The leaves are thick and leathery, in the shape of love hearts, approximately 6cm (2¼in) wide, 5mm (¼in) thick. Seen here as a single, heart-shaped leaf planted in a pot, it stays unchanged for many months, then will grow quickly in a year or so up to 1m (3ft).

In the summer, adult plants produce unusual, star-shaped, cream and blood-red flowers on globe-shaped hanging umbels.

KALANCHOE THYRSIFLORA

ETYMOLOGY

Thyrsiflora refers to the inflorescence, which is a "thryse", or many-flowered variety.

Its common names include paddle plant and desert cabbage, but the Afrikaans name, *meelplakkie,* is perhaps the most appropriate, as it does indeed look as if the whole plant has been liberally dusted with flour (*meel*).

PROFILE

Kalanchoe thyrsiflora is native to South Africa. It's formed of a rosette of large, rounded, slightly concave, pale green leaves with a whitish coating and red margin. The chalky coating on the leaves and inflorescence helps to reflect the sun, thus keeping the plant cool. It grows to a height of about 35cm (14in).

The flowering stalk, about 1m (3ft) tall, bears heavily scented, brilliant yellow flowers with a cylindrical flower tube and broadly obovate (egg-shaped) lobes in spring. It dies back after flowering.

These plants will survive neglect. Overwatering is the most common cause of plant failure, so be careful with that water! Avoid getting the leaves wet, too, to prevent rot.

LITHOPS

ETYMOLOGY

The name is derived from the Greek *lithos*, meaning "stone", and *ops*, meaning "face" – a theme that carries into its common names of flowering stones and living stones.

PROFILE

The first scientific description of a *Lithops* was in 1811 by botanist and artist William John Burchell, who accidentally found a specimen when picking up a "curiously shaped pebble" from the ground.

Native to Southern Africa, these plants avoid being eaten by camouflaging themselves to look like surrounding rocks, hence their common name of living stones. Plants develop a new pair of leaves each year. The leaf markings of any one plant change very little from year to year, and no two plants have the same markings – a little like fingerprints.

They survive the scorching heat of their native lands by living mostly underground, with only the top surface of their leaves exposed. In times of drought, the leaves may shrink and disappear altogether below ground level.

During the summer months, they become dormant, flowering at the end of the growing season, which is usually autumn. Blooms emerge between the leaves, with some species having flowers large enough to obscure the leaves entirely. They open in the afternoon and close in the evening.

After flowering, the furrow between the leaves splits, revealing a new set of leaves perpendicular to the old ones. From this moment onwards, the plant *must* be kept bone dry, only watered once the old leaves have completely dried up. The new body continues to extract the water and nutrients stored in the old leaves – if watering commences before the old leaves have dried up, the plant will die.

These plants require a certain amount of direct sunlight, otherwise they will begin to grow slender and elongated and lean to one side.

LITHOPS AUCAMPIAE

ETYMOLOGY
Named after Juanita Aucamp, who discovered this species on her father's farm in Postmasburg, Northern Cape, in 1929. It is most commonly known as living stone, mimicry plant or stone plant.

PROFILE
Lithops aucampiae (the brown example in the photograph above) is found in South Africa, where it lives among stones and gravel. Characterized by the classic *Lithops* structure of two very thick, fleshy, semi-circular leaves separated by a shallow fissure, this species also has a large leaf "window" to allow light to penetrate right into the plant.

From late summer to early autumn, a yellow flower grows from the fissure separating the two leaves.

The photograph above also shows *Lithops lesliei* "Albinica" (the smaller green plants). Named after Thomas Nicholas Leslie, whose son, Owen, discovered the plant in 1908, this variety features a translucent "window" on each leaf tip. Its large, white, daisy-like flowers emerge in early autumn.

MAMMILLARIA

ETYMOLOGY

The first species of this cactus was described by the 18th-century Swedish botanist Carl Linnaeus as *Cactus mammillaris* in 1753. The name is derived from the Latin *mamma*, meaning "teat", referring to the distinctive tubercles, but also *mammilla*, meaning "breast", referencing the shape of many of the species. The common name for the genus is pincushion cactus.

PROFILE

Mammillaria is one of the most popular and most studied genera of cacti, and there are currently around 200 known species. Nearly all of them are native to Mexico, but a handful are also found in the United States, Colombia, Venezuela, Guatemala, Honduras and the West Indies.

These cacti are usually small, low-growing and spiny, with globose to elongated stems and many prominent tubercles. Although solitary, some will clump to form huge mounds.

The funnel-shaped flowers range in colour from white and greenish to yellow, pink and red, often with a darker central stripe, and are typically located in a ring near the apex of the stem, forming a halo shape.

MAMMILLARIA
BACKEBERGIANA
(SYN. MAMMILLARIA ERNESTII)

ETYMOLOGY

The name is in honour the German horticulturist Curt Backeberg.

PROFILE

Mammillaria backebergiana originates from Mexico. Characterized by slender spines on green stems with pronounced tubercles, this cactus reaches a maximum height of 30cm (12in). In the spring or summer, purplish red or white flowers sprout in several rings at the apex of the stem. This cactus blooms easily and in abundance, making it a favourite for new collectors.

MAMMILLARIA BOMBYCINA

ETYMOLOGY

Commonly known as silken pincushion cactus due to their thin, hooked spines.

PROFILE

Native to western Central Mexico, this cactus is characterized by green, columnar stems reaching 20cm (8in) in height, which clump to form huge mounds. The stem body is almost completely hidden by fine white spines with a long, hooked reddish/golden brown central spine. Only mature plants flower in the spring/summer, producing pink or white flowers.

MAMMILLARIA HAHNIANA

ETYMOLOGY
Commonly known as old lady cactus.

PROFILE
This is a spherical or slightly columnar cactus, densely covered with white, hair-like spines. They can be found growing solo or forming clusters reaching 20cm (8in) in height. It flowers in the spring/summer with pink flowers, which form a halo on the apex of the stem.

MAMMILLARIA MAGNIMAMMA
(SYN. MAMMILLARIA ZUCCARINIANA)

ETYMOLOGY

Commonly known as the Mexican pincushion.

PROFILE

Native to Mexico, this plant grows largely in rocky terrain.
The plants are solitary at first, but later branch basally to form
large mounds up to 1m (3ft) in diameter.

In the spring/summer months, the grey-green, columnar-shaped
stems produce a ring of flowers at their apex in a range of
cream, red or pink colours.

MATUCANA MADISONIORUM
(SYN. SUBMATUCANA MADISONIORUM)

ETYMOLOGY

This cactus is native to a single restricted area of dry forest, roughly 16km² (6sq mi) in area, in the Amazonas region of northern Peru. It takes its name from the nearby town of Matucana. The species name comes from a certain Marshall P. Madison.

PROFILE

This small, solitary, globose cactus will eventually grow to about 15cm (6in) tall and reach 10cm (4in) in diameter. It may also clump with age.

One of its appealing features is its unusual, rough-textured, blue or grey-green body with subtle ribs. Individual plants may be entirely spineless or covered with spines, or have some spines missing. Spineless plants are often confused with another cactus, *Lophophora williamsii* (peyote).

Plants can bloom several times in summer, producing bright orange-red flowers. They have a tendency to lean to one side. They benefit from good but not severe sunlight, with a minimum temperature of 10°C (50°F).

MIQUELIOPUNTIA MIQUELII
(SYN. OPUNTIA MIQUELII)

ETYMOLOGY

The name of this cactus honours Dr Friedrich Anton Wilhelm Miquel, the 19th-century Dutch physician and botanist and director of the botanical gardens of Rotterdam, Amsterdam and Utrecht.

PROFILE

Native to the Chilean coast of South America, *Miqueliopuntia miquelii* is the only species of cactus in its genus. It is an uncommon, heavily branched, upright, bushy plant. Usually less than 1m (3ft) high, it has elongated, cylindrical, bluish joints and younger bright green joints. Its spines are needle-like and very unequal in size.

Large flowers – almost white to pink – bloom at adult stage, when the plant is up to 50 years old, in early summer, often after decades. It is said that some plants have not flowered for the first 50 years of their lives.

NEOBUXBAUMIA POLYLOPHA

ETYMOLOGY

The genus name honours the 20th-century Austrian botantist Franz Buxbaum. The prefix *neo*, meaning "new", was added because a moss with the name *Buxbaumia* already existed. *Polylopha* comes from the Greek for "many crests", referring to the plant's ribs. It goes by the more common names of cone cactus, golden saguaro, golden spined saguaro and wax cactus.

PROFILE

Native to a small area (less than 6km² (2¼sq miles) of canyons with limestone slopes in the state of Guanajuato, Mexico, *Neobuxbaumia polylopha* is a very tall, thick, columnar, green-stemmed cactus. Characterized by a high number of narrow ribs, it can grow to heights of over 15m (49ft) and weigh many tonnes.

The flowers bloom at night in summer at heights upwards of 3m (10ft) on the stem, growing on most of the areoles in deep shades of red. Unusually for such columnar cacti, which tend to have white flowers, these are red in colour. They open up during the day and are pollinated by insects. Although intolerant of the cold, these cacti are easy to cultivate, and can grow up to 15–20cm (6–8in) a year.

OPUNTIA

ETYMOLOGY

Opuntia is named after the Ancient Greek region of Locris Opuntia, whose capital city was called Opus. According to Theophrastus, considered the grandfather of botany, an edible prickly plant grew there, which could be propagated by rooting its leaves.

PROFILE

The genus *Opuntia* is native to only the Americas, but it quickly became naturalized in parts of Europe (Spain and areas of the Mediterranean) and also North Africa after it was first discovered by European explorers in the 16th century.

It is one of the most common, popular and widespread genera of cacti, characterized by a lack of stem and flat, pad-like segments that multiply quickly. Some species are spineless, while others have a polka-dot pattern of tufts of glochids at the areoles dotted over the body of the plant. Some have very long, prominent spines.

Species in this genus range from small groundcover plants to large tropical trees.

The *Opuntia* genus is the most cold-tolerant of the lowland cacti groups.

OPUNTIA POLYACANTHA VAR. ERINACEA

ETYMOLOGY

Polyacantha, from the Greek, means "many spines"; *erinacea*, "like a hedgehog". It is commonly known as the Mojave prickly pear, grizzly bear prickly pear or hedgehog prickly pear.

PROFILE

This cactus is native to the Mojave and Great Basin deserts of the United States. Growing to a maximum height of 45cm (18in), the plant is formed of stem segments bearing characteristic whisker-like spines, up to 10cm (4in) in length, which give the plant a shaggy, hairy appearance. It produces light yellow flowers with reddish tips in summer. A hardy plant, it can withstand temperatures down to at least -20°C (-4°F).

OPUNTIA FICUS-INDICA

ETYMOLOGY

The Latin *ficus*, meaning "fig", relates to the plant's edible fruit, and *indica*, meaning "from India", to its origins in the West Indies (originally believed to be a part of India). It's more commonly known as a prickly pear or Indian fig.

PROFILE

In spite of its name, *Opuntia ficus-indica* is thought to have originated in Mexico, where it is known as nopal. It is a shrubby or tree-like cactus, which can grow up to 6m (20ft) tall. The stem segments into large, green/greyish pads, with inconsistent or a complete absence of spines.

The plant's flowers range in colour from white and yellow through to red, and appear in spring and summer. *Opuntia ficus-indica* is, however, grown primarily as a fruit crop commercially, rather than as an ornamental plant. The fruits have a taste similar to sweet watermelon, and the bright red or white/yellowish flesh contains many tiny hard seeds.

OPUNTIA MICRODASYS

ETYMOLOGY

This plant takes its species name from the Greek *mikros*, meaning "small", and *dasys*, meaning "dense" or "rough", for the fine dense glochids and absence of spines.

Its common names include white bunny ears, rabbit ears cactus, bunny ears cactus, bunny cactus, polka-dot cactus, angel's wings and bunny-ear prickly pear.

PROFILE

Native to central and northern Mexico, this plant forms a dense shrub, 40–60cm (16–24in) tall, with no central stem or leaves. It is composed of pad-like stems, with new segments growing in pairs, giving the appearance of bunny ears. Instead of spines, it has numerous white or yellow glochids, 2–3mm (about ⅛in) long, in dense clusters. These detach in large numbers upon the slightest touch and will cause considerable skin irritation.

In the summer, plants produce lemon-yellow flowers, 3–5cm (1–2in) in diameter, which sprout from the terminal ends of the segment pads. They are easy to propagate from any fully grown pad (see page 190).

OPUNTIA MONACANTHA

ETYMOLOGY
Common names for this plant include drooping prickly pear, cochineal prickly pear and Barbary fig.

PROFILE
Opuntia monacantha is an odd, shrubby or tree-like plant, characterized by its long, smooth, flattened green body that forms curious, monstrous shapes, appearing stretched, with creamy green, elongated, drooping stems covered in tiny, hair-like spines. Yellow flowers appear along the edges of the most lateral pads in late winter and early spring.

Reaching a maximum height of 1m (3ft), it is a fast-growing species that branches profusely from the side and near the tips, and can reach a height of 50–100cm (20in–3ft) in just a few years, given the best conditions.

The variegated form of *Opuntia monacantha*, *Opuntia monacantha* var. *variegata*, is one of the few naturally variegated cacti. It bears small, fine, pink-purple spines with small red flowers.

OREOCEREUS

ETYMOLOGY

The name *Oreocereus* loosely means "mountain cactus". It is derived from the Greek *oreo*, meaning "mountain", and the Latin *cereus*, meaning "waxy" or "candle", referencing the genus *Cereus*. However, because of its appearance, it is also commonly known as old man cactus.

PROFILE

These cacti originate in the high altitudes of the Andes in South America. They are characterized by their short, columnar stature and covering of thick, white wool, or hair, with sharp spines hiding underneath. These woolly hairs provide shade from the increased radiation and heat from the sun in the mountains.

On summer days these plants produce single flowers with tube-shaped funnels near the stem apexes.

OREOCEREUS TROLLII

ETYMOLOGY

Named after the 20th-century German botany professor Wilhelm Troll, *Oreocereus trollii* is also known as the old man of the Andes.

PROFILE

This shrubby columnar cactus has fine, white, completely all-encompassing hair and powerful, red-coloured spines.

Pink, tubular flowers appear in the summer.

PACHYPHYTUM OVIFERUM

ETYMOLOGY

The genus name *Pachyphytum* comes from the Greek *pachys*, meaning "thick", and *phyton*, meaning "plant" or "tree", so it therefore translates to something like "fat plant". *Oviferum* is derived from the Latin *ovum*, meaning "egg", and *fero*, for "to carry/bear". Its more common names are moonstones and sugar almond plant.

PROFILE

Native to northern Mexico, this rather attractive, short, shrubby succulent is characterized by a loose rosette of very plump, pale blue, flattened egg-shaped leaves with a powdery coating, which creates a pearlescent effect. The natural oils in our skin are harmful to the leaves, so avoid handling them.

In the spring and summer this species produces a tall stem sprouting delicate, bell-shaped, greenish-white and pink or deep red flowers.

This cactus can stand high temperatures and direct sunlight, but will not tolerate frost and is best kept above 7°C (45°F). When thirsty, the leaves will appear wilted and wrinkled.

PARODIA

ETYMOLOGY

This genus of cactus is named after the 19th-century Italian botanist Domingo Parodi, one of the early documenters of Paraguayan flora.

PROFILE

Natives of Paraguay, Argentina, Peru, Bolivia, Brazil, Colombia and Uruguay, these cacti are generally easy to grow and relatively small in size, making them particularly suitable for indoor planting. They flower well with brightly coloured blooms.

PARODIA AUREICENTRA

ETYMOLOGY

The Latin *aureus*, meaning "yellow", and *centrum*, meaning "centre", for the colour of the central spines, is the etymology behind this species name.

PROFILE

Parodia aureicentra is a solitary-growing cactus that is globose in shape, with a heavily ribbed, bright green stem, and grows to a height of 50cm (20in). It is defined by its dark yellow, brown to black, hooked spines. Yellow or bright red flowers are produced in summer.

PARODIA LENINGHAUSII
(SYN. NOTOCACTUS LENINGHAUSII)

ETYMOLOGY

This cactus was formally named in honour of the 19th-century Brazilian cactus collector Guillermo Leninghaus. It is commonly known as the golden ball cactus.

PROFILE

Like *Parodia warasii* (see page 141), this species originates from Rio Grande do Sul, Brazil. Although it can be a solitary grower, it is more often found in clumps. The stems are green and columnar, reaching 60cm (2ft) in height, and are covered in golden yellow, bristly spines. In the summer mature plants produce silky, lemon-yellow flowers, with beautiful shiny petals.

PARODIA MAGNIFICA
(SYN. NOTOCACTUS MAGNIFICUS)

ETYMOLOGY

This "magnificent" species of *Parodia* is commonly known as balloon cactus, green ball cactus and blue ball cactus.

PROFILE

Native to the Rio Grande do Sul region in Brazil, *Parodia magnifica* is a geometric globular cactus, becoming short and cylindrical with age, that grows in clusters. These cacti develop a slight depression at the apex with bristly yellow spines gracing the ribs. Plants are at first solitary, reaching 30cm (12in) in height and 7–15cm (2½–6in) across, but form large, clustering mounds over time.

Plants will bloom several times in summer through to early autumn, producing many funnel-shaped, brilliant sulphur-yellow flowers at a time.

PARODIA OTTONIS
(SYN. NOTOCACTUS OTTONIS)

ETYMOLOGY

The name of Christoph Friedrich Otto, a 19th-century German botanist, is behind this species of *Parodia*.

PROFILE

This is a popular plant for collectors because it is easy to cultivate and also flowers at a young age. A very attractive cactus, it is a deep green and more or less spherical. Slender, hair-like spines sparsely populate the rib edges. It produces bright, satiny yellow flowers from the crown in summer.

It is hardy to -5°C (23°F) for short periods of time.

PARODIA WARASII
(SYN. NOTOCACTUS WARASII)

ETYMOLOGY

Named in honour of Eddie Waras, a plant collector, this cactus originates specifically from Rio Grande do Sul, in Brazil.

PROFILE

This green, globular cactus is prone to forming clumps. Stems become tall and erect as the plant matures, reaching up to 60cm (2ft) tall, 30cm (12in) in diameter. Its spines are golden yellow, forming bright rows down its ribs. The large, yellow flowers with glossy petals are borne from the apex of the stem and appear during summer.

Easy to grow, *Parodia warasii* likes a warm, bright location, but avoid full sun. It performs very well in partial shade and is happiest above 0°C (32°F). Keep on the dry side in winter.

PEPEROMIA ASPERULA

ETYMOLOGY

This genus name is derived from the Greek words *peperi*, meaning "pepper", and *homoios*, for "similar". The species name is from the Latin *asperus*, meaning "somewhat rough", for the textured leaves.

PROFILE

Native to subtropical regions of South and Central America, *Peperomia* is a large genus of 500 or more plants, with only a handful belonging to the succulent family. *Peperomia asperula* is a compact, small succulent formed of dark green stems covered with thick, folded leaves with a light green, velvety underside.

Reaching a mature height of 1m (3ft), *Peperomia asperula* does not bear flowers.

PILOSOCEREUS PACHYCLADUS
(SYN. P. AZUREUS)

ETYMOLOGY

Pilosocereus is derived from the Latin words *pilosus*, meaning "hairy", and *cereus*, meaning "waxy" or "candle". The species name is made up of the Greek *pachy*, meaning "thick", and *cladus*, meaning "branch". Its common name is the tree cactus.

PROFILE

Originating in Brazil, this is one of the most spectacular examples in the genus, its columnar, tree-like body reaching 10m (30ft) in height. It is notable for its sky-blue or bluish-silver stem that branches at the base or develops a distinct trunk with dozens of branches. The blue stems are lined with hairy areoles emitting golden spines.

The funnel-shaped flowers, whitish with greenish or reddish outer segments, open at night in summer and continue the day after. However, flowers are seen only on large, mature specimens that are at least 1m (3ft) tall.

PLEIOSPILOS NELII

ETYMOLOGY

The Greek words *pleios*, meaning "full", and *spilos*, meaning "dots", referring to the dots covering the plants, are behind the genus name. The species name *nelii* is in honour of the South African Gert Cornelius Nel, a 20th-century professor of botany. The common names are split rock plant, liver plant and stone plant.

PROFILE

This native to South Africa is an intriguing little succulent and one of the best examples of mimicry in botany. Resembling a rock, it is a dwarf, stem-less plant with two or four opposing, grey-green, well-speckled, near-hemispherical leaves. Flowers emerge from the centre of the leaves, and are large in relation to the size of the plant. They bloom in the afternoon and close at sunset. The flowering period extends from early spring to late summer.

In the winter, it grows new leaves from the centre of the split, and the new leaves then consume the old leaves. If the plant is overwatered, the old leaves remain and the plant usually rots and dies. The key is not to water when it is splitting, but to leave it alone. The cycle is just like that of *Lithops* (see page 116). *Pleiospilos nelii* does best on a sunny windowsill.

POLASKIA CHICHIPE

ETYMOLOGY

This species is named after Charles and Mary Polaski, two
20th-century American cactus enthusiasts. Its Mexican vernacular
name is behind the species name.

PROFILE

Native to central Mexico, *Polaskia chichipe* is a columnar,
tree-like cactus. Noted for its greenish and powdery-grey stem
with striations and many curved branches, it can grow up to
5m (16ft) tall, though it usually has a short trunk, around 1m (3ft).
This species has yellowish green to white flowers that open at
night in spring and summer.

RHIPSALIS

ETYMOLOGY

Named from the Greek word *rhips*, which means "wickerwork", referring to the slender, flexible, reed-like stems, this genus was first described by the German botanist Joseph Gaertner in 1788.

PROFILE

There are just under 40 species of *Rhipsalis*. They are widespread in South America, up into Central America and as far as the Caribbean, but most occur in the tropical rainforests of Brazil. There is even one species present in Madagascar and Sri Lanka, which is the only cactus that occurs naturally outside the New World.

Most plants have pendent stems, but there are a few that are more or less upright or sprawling in habit. There are three main stem shapes: terete, angular and flattened. Spines are generally absent, but when present, they are very fine and hair-like.

Their flowers are among the smallest of all cactus flowers, usually about 1cm (½in) in diameter and predominantly white, though some may have a yellow or red tinge. The fruits are always berries, and coloured either whitish, pink, red or yellow.

In the wild, *Rhipsalis* is accustomed to receiving light that has been filtered through dense, overhanging tree branches. Direct exposure to sunlight can burn the leaves or turn them yellow, so keep plants at least 50cm (20in) away from windows that receive midday or afternoon sun. They will do best with morning sun and full shade in the afternoon.

RHIPSALIS BACCIFERA

ETYMOLOGY

The species name is taken from the Latin word *baca*, meaning "berry", and *ferrer*, "to bear". Its common name is mistletoe cactus.

PROFILE

This is one of the most popular *Rhipsalis* species. Graceful in habit, it has long, thread-like stems, and produces many creamy white flowers in winter or spring. These are followed by mistletoe-like berries, which are usually white or pale pink. The plant can reach a height of 1–4m (3–13ft).

SANSEVIERIA

ETYMOLOGY

This genus is named for Raimondo di Sangro, the 18th-century prince of San Severo, Italy, and a scholar. Its common names include mother-in-law's tongue, devil's tongue, jinn's tongue, bowstring hemp, snake plant and snake tongue.

PROFILE

Sansevieria is a genus of about 70 species of succulent plants, native to subtropical Africa, Madagascar and southern Asia. All species can be divided into one of two categories based on their leaves: hard-leaved (desert natives) and soft-leaved (tropical plants).

Indoors, they thrive on warmth and bright light, but also tolerate shade and humidity, hence their "indestructible" reputation.

SANSEVIERIA TRIFASCIATA

ETYMOLOGY

The species name comes from the Latin *tres*, meaning "three", and *fascis*, for "bundle", referring to the colour bands on the leaves.

PROFILE

This tall succulent reaches up to 1m (3ft) in height. Its dense, stiff leaves grow vertically from a basal rosette and are dark green with light grey-green cross-banding and yellow margins.

Sansevieria trifasciata has a well-deserved reputation for indestructibility, and is also popular for its air-filtering ability. A NASA Clean Air Study found that it purifies air by removing toxins such as formaldehyde, xylene and toluene. The plant uses the CAM (Crassulacean Acid Metabolism) process (see page 16), which absorbs carbon dioxide and releases oxygen at night, making it particularly beneficial in the bedroom.

SCHLUMBERGERA

ETYMOLOGY

Named after the 19th-century French cactus collector Frederic Schlumberger, this plant has the common name of Christmas cactus. It's so-called because it flowers from late autumn to mid-winter, meaning that it makes a wonderful Christmas display and an ideal gift for the season.

PROFILE

The genus occurs only in the coastal mountains of southeast Brazil, primarily the Serra dos Órgãos (Organ Mountains). Because of their height and proximity to the Atlantic Ocean, these coastal mountains are home to moist, jungle-like woodland at a high altitude, where these plants grow naturally on trees or rocks. They prefer cool partial shade with high humidity, as opposed to the full sun enjoyed by desert-dwelling cacti. Too much exposure to sun or heat can cause the leaves to shrivel or discolour.

Schlumbergera is a small genus comprising just six species. Most have stems resembling leaf-like pads, and tubular flowers, which appear from the corners and tips of the stems in autumn and winter. In the wild, these flowers, with their abundant nectar and brightly coloured petals, encourage pollination by hummingbirds. Flower colours range from white, yellow, orange, pink and purple to cherry-red.

Plants in the genus require two rest periods, when they should not be watered: after flowering in winter to early spring, then again in early autumn after the flowering buds start to develop (see pages 174–175).

SCHLUMBERGERA TRUNCATA

ETYMOLOGY

Latin for "truncated", the species name relates to the shape of this plant's leaves, which are cut off instead of pointed.

PROFILE

Schlumbergera truncata, also known as the false Christmas cactus, has square- or rectangular-shaped stems resembling leaf-like pads and bears tubular flowers, which appear from the corners and tips of the stems from autumn to winter.

SEDUM MORGANIANUM

ETYMOLOGY

The species salutes Dr Meredith W. Morgan (1887–1957), an American enthusiast of all things succulent. The common name is donkey tail or burro's tail.

PROFILE

Native to southern Mexico and Honduras, this succulent is characterized by overlapping, lance-shaped, fleshy, trailing stems that grow up to 60cm (2ft) long. The leaves are also fleshy and blue-green. Pink to red flowers are produced in summer.

It is a popular choice for growing indoors, where it makes a very attractive hanging plant. It is best placed in full sunlight for strong growth and to enhance leaf coloration, but avoid exposing to extreme heat, as it is prone to drying out.

SEMPERVIVUM

ETYMOLOGY

Sempervivum is derived from the Latin *semper*, meaning "always", and *vivus*, for "living", referencing this succulent's evergreen status. Its common name is houseleek, which is derived from the traditional practice of growing these plants on rooftops to ward off fire or lightning strikes.

PROFILE

This genus, native to the mountainous regions of Europe and Asia, forms dense mats of foliage, with thick, pointed leaves. Easy to care for, almost thriving on neglect, certain species are used today as "green roofs".

SEMPERVIVUM ARACHNOIDEUM

ETYMOLOGY

"Arachnoid" in botany is a term used to describe something cobweb-like in appearance, and comes from the Greek *arakhnē*, meaning "spider". The common name is cobweb houseleek.

PROFILE

Sempervivum arachnoideum is a lime-green, fleshy, rosette-forming succulent covered in a cobweb-like wool. Growing to 8cm (3in) tall and 30cm (12in) wide, it is valued in cultivation for its ability to cluster quickly with offsets (see page 188). It blooms in mid-summer, with star-shaped, pink flowers that are raised on stems.

SEMPERVIVUM TECTORUM 'GREENII'

ETYMOLOGY

Tectorum is Latin for "of roofs"; *greenii* speaks for itself. Hens and chicks is the common name. This plant is also known as *Sempervivum calcereum* 'Greenii'.

PROFILE

This succulent is native to the mountainous regions of southern Europe. It is a rosette-forming evergreen perennial, growing up to 15cm (6in) tall and spreading quickly by growing offsets (see page 188). It has grey-green, textured leaves, which are flat and form rosettes with red edges. In summer it produces clusters of reddish-purple flowers.

SENECIO

ETYMOLOGY

Senex, meaning "old man" in Latin, is the root of the genus name and refers to the hairy parts of the flowers.

PROFILE

The *Senecio* genus, which contains more than 1,000 species, includes succulents from tropical and subtropical areas all over the world. Requiring little maintenance, members of this genus make ideal houseplants.

SENECIO ROWLEYANUS

ETYMOLOGY

Named in 1921 for Gordon D. Rowley, an English botantist specializing in succulents, this plant also goes by the names of string of pearls, rosary pearls, bead plant, string of peas, string of marbles, necklace plant, string of beads, green peas and rosary vine.

PROFILE

Originating from the Eastern and Western Cape provinces of South Africa, and southern Namibia, this succulent is formed of very slender, thin, wiry, green stems that carry globular, pearl-shaped leaves along them. In its natural habitat the plant will grow creeping shoots that form a mat along the ground.

These plants are perfect for placing on sunny windowsills or planting in hanging baskets, and will rapidly form long, dense bunches of thin stems dangling over the edge of a pot. They prefer warmer environments.

Senecio herreianus is a very similar plant – the main difference is that it has thicker stems, and the leaves are larger, less globular and more teardrop-shaped.

SENECIO STAPELIIFORMIS
(SYN. KLEINIA STAPELIIFORMIS)

ETYMOLOGY

The etymology of this species is a combination of *Stapelia*, a genus of succulents, and the Latin *formis*, relating to shape, indicating that *Senecio stapeliiformis* resembles the *Stapelia* genus. Common names include pickle plant, inch worm, candle stick and candle plant.

PROFILE

Originating in Kenya and Tanzania, *Senecio stapeliiformis* is an attractive succulent with soft, pencil-like stems, 2–25cm (¾–10in) long. It has tinted, scale-like leaves along the ribs, patterned with a silvery-green striation.

It is a fast-growing plant, with stems that can travel underground before emerging. It flowers in late spring/early summer, sprouting a very delicate and dainty red/orange flower from the tips of the stems.

STENOCACTUS CRISPATUS
(SYN. ECHINOFOSSULOCACTUS GUERRAIANUS)

ETYMOLOGY

Stenocactus derives from the Greek *stenos*, meaning "narrow", referring to the plant's narrow ribs, while *crispatus* is Latin for "wavy edged".

PROFILE

The wavy-edged, yellow-green to dark matt green, globular stem, adorned with many narrow ribs in an almost concertina shape, proves to be this plant's most defining feature, together with the yellow/brown, flat, dagger-shaped spines. The plant grows to a maximum height and spread of 8cm (3in).

Originating from Hidalgo, Mexico, this cactus is very willing to flower, producing multiple blooms in spring from the tip of the stem in a deep pink-purple, with pale pink or white outer edges.

TEPHROCACTUS ARTICULATUS VAR. PAPYRACANTHUS

ETYMOLOGY

The species name means "jointed", from the Latin *articulare*, "to divide into joints". *Papyracanthus* indicates that the cactus has paper-like spines. Paper spine cactus is a common name.

PROFILE

Native to western Argentina, this cactus grows pinecone-shaped segments vertically like a string of beads. It doesn't usually get to be very tall, as its segments have a habit of falling apart, resulting in a maximum height of 30cm (12in).

Some *Tephrocactus articulatus* have spines, while others have none at all. The former are also known as *papyracanthus*, due to their unusual, soft, wide, flattened, raffia-like spines. Plants vary in colour, markings and length, and have small glochids at their base, which are hard to see but will definitely be felt, so handle with care. Blooms are either white or yellow.

It is fairly cold resistant and hardy to -9°C (16°F). Propagation is usually done with cuttings; stem segments easily break away and can be popped straight into the compost (see page 188).

PLANT GALLERY & DIRECTORY

CARE GUIDE

INTRODUCTION

To keep our cacti and succulents happy and healthy, it's important to replicate their natural environment as best we can in our homes. Even though these plants are tougher and less demanding than other houseplants, it's a popular misconception that they are impossible to kill. It can be done – usually through extreme neglect or overwatering.

The following is a basic guide to caring for your cacti and succulents, covering such topics as providing the right growing conditions, watering and repotting. I've also included some tips and ideas about how to make the best of these plants' unique qualities in your home.

LIGHT & TEMPERATURE

The majority of cacti and succulents have adapted over thousands of years to live in warm, dry climates. As plant owners, our aim is to try to replicate their natural environment to help them flourish in our homes. Greenhouses or conservatories are ideal, as they offer all-round light. However, that kind of space is a luxury that we can't all enjoy, especially the city dwellers among us. But a sunny windowsill will usually do the job – although some succulents do prefer half-shade (see the relevant entry in the Plant Gallery & Directory, pages 28–165). Be sure to rotate your plants every couple of weeks to prevent them from leaning towards the light.

Cacti and succulents require good ventilation during the summer months.

When plants are enclosed in our homes, it is hard for them to be aware of the seasons, as they would in their natural habitat. That means it is important for us to replicate the growing and dormant seasons for them: the former is early spring to mid-autumn, and the latter, mid-autumn to early spring.

From mid-autumn to early spring, keep your succulents and cacti in a cool position in the home: that is, not above a radiator or

other heat source, but at a temperature no lower than a comfortable 7°C (44°F).

Central heating in our homes provides a warm and dry environment, which is perfect for these plants. However, in the dormant season this can cause them to continue growing, instead of enjoying their winter's rest. It's important to try to mimic the plants' natural environment so they can follow their natural rhythms and – all being well – provide you with beautiful flowers, right on cue.

DIAGNOSING THE PROBLEM

Like any living thing, cacti and succulents can fall victim to a fairly wide range of ailments and illnesses, which aren't always easy to tell apart. To help you assess the damage, here is a guide to the most common signs of poor health:

• **Growing to a point or into a disfigured shape (see right) is usually caused by a lack of light.**

• **Skin wrinkling in winter is natural contraction and generally nothing to worry about.**

• **Discoloration on the sun-facing side of a plant is a sign of scorching.** The plant needs to be rotated or moved to a less sunny spot.

• **A discoloured band on the plant stem usually signifies cold damage, meaning that the plant has been subjected to temperatures that are lower than ideal.**

• **A fluffy white substance on the leaves is the sign of a small common pest called mealybugs.** They are often found on houseplants, but are especially fond of cacti and succulents. A dab of rubbing alcohol or methylated spirits can remove them. It is also a good idea to use an insecticide aerosol spray twice a year for those plants prone to them. Bear in mind, though, that the overuse of insecticides can actually attract bugs to the plant.

• **If the plant is severely shrivelled and looks brown, black or white, this is pretty bad news, and generally means RIP plant.**

WATERING

To imitate the natural habitat of cacti during their native winter, try to keep them as dry as possible by not watering from mid-autumn to early spring; this is their enforced winter rest, where plants should be kept in a dry, cool and airy place. Having said that, given the extra warmth provided by central heating, it's a good idea to lightly water or spray plants once a month to prevent their roots from drying up.

Early spring is the time to start watering most succulents but it needs to be done gradually. Increase your light watering to once a week by late spring and continue throughout the summer. Allow the soil to dry between waterings but remember that smaller pots dry out faster than large ones.

Feed every four to six weeks, using a succulent-specific feed – see page 176 – during the growing season (early spring to mid-autumn).

I'm often asked exactly how much I water our plants – I say "thoroughly", so that you see the water drain out of the pot. Then water again only when the soil has completely dried out.

From early autumn you should start to reduce the watering to prepare for the winter – it is not good to just stop suddenly. This allows the plants to harden their tissues and become more inactive ahead of the dormant winter period. If they are kept active, they will be in no condition to withstand low temperatures and winter humidity.

FEEDING

Succulents require a different ratio of
nutrients – nitrogen (N), phosphorus (P)
and potassium (K) – to regular houseplants,
so a specific cactus or succulent feed can
really aid growth during the active growing
season. Most good garden stores should
stock them. Remember not to use feed
during a plant's winter break.

REPOTTING

Repotting is a necessary part of a plant's life – just like a hermit crab outgrows its shell, so a plant can outgrow its surroundings and need to move to new digs. The process can be daunting for the novice but it really doesn't need to be. The simple instructions below should help.

When do you need to repot?

• Over time the nutrients in the soil will be consumed. Young plants in particular may require a change in compost every year.

• A plant can quickly outgrow its pot and require upsizing.

• Your plant might look unhappy but you aren't sure why – this may be caused by one of the reasons above, or you may need to repot in order to inspect the roots to find out the cause.

Key things to remember

• If a plant is happy, healthy and growing, there's no need to stress it out. Let it do its thing and don't disturb it by repotting.

• The best time to repot is soon after the plant starts to grow in the spring.

• Wait two weeks after repotting to water.

• Large plants can be repotted every 3–4 years.

TOOLS

Gardening gloves

Old paintbrush

Plastic plant pot

Compost

Tablespoon

Horticultural grit or decorative gravel

Noose made of newspaper

Long nose pliers

HOW TO REPOT YOUR PLANTS

1. Put on your gloves and place the plant on its side.

2. Use the end of the paintbrush to push the plant out of its pot through the drainage holes.

3. Remove as much compost as possible from the rootball with your fingers.

4. Select the most appropriately sized pot for repotting.

5. Add compost to the pot so that the plant will sit at the right height, with its neck just below the edge of the pot.

6. Put the plant inside the new pot.

7. Use the tablespoon to apply compost to cover the roots, tapping the side of the pot to make sure the compost fills all of the spaces below.

8. Use the handle of the tablespoon to push the compost down around the edge of the pot.

9. Cover the top of the compost with grit – this is both for decorative purposes and to prevent the compost from drying out.

When handling very spiky cacti use a folded piece of newspaper to create a noose with which to safely pick up the plant. You can also use long nose pliers to lift the plant pot.

COMPOST

Cacti and succulents like an open, gritty compost that will allow surplus water to drain through easily. There are many different substrates you can use to create free-draining compost – many collectors choose to add kitty litter. There are some succulents that require specific compost and this should be researched before repotting.

At Prick, we use a basic succulent compost, which is a 1:1:1 compound of the following ingredients, all of which should be readily available at a garden store:

1 part pumice
1 part John Innes no.2 compost
1 part coir compost

The only problem with using compost like this is that it isn't the most attractive thing in the world to look at – so you may want to top your compost with a little gravel. This not only makes the plant more aesthetically pleasing but also prevents the top soil from drying out.

SPECIAL CARE

Lithops (see page 116) are worthy of particular mention in this section, as they are very particular plants which, if you follow a few basic rules, can truly thrive in the home.

They perform well if they receive about 4–5 hours of direct sunlight during the early part of the day, and partial shade for the afternoon. Therefore, an east-facing windowsill is ideal. If plants don't get adequate direct sunlight, they will begin to grow slender and elongated, leaning to one side in their search for more light, and they can also lose coloration. This will eventually kill the plant over time.

Watering is another important consideration that must be taken into account. *Lithops* have a specific yearly cycle of growth and it is important to withhold water until the outside leaves completely dry up (see pages 174–175).

PROPAGATING

Plant propagation is the process of creating new plants from a variety of sources: seeds, cuttings, bulbs and other parts of a plant. When we do this ourselves, it means more plants at no extra cost.

It is always such a joy to see our plants grow and flourish, and we get an added sense of achievement when they multiply. Succulents are especially good at this, producing offsets or replicating themselves from cuttings.

PROPAGATING FROM SUCCULENT LEAVES, SUCH AS ECHEVERIA OR SEDUM

Detach a leaf from the parent plant using your fingers, or take a fallen leaf, and lay it on dry compost with the base of the leaf pointing downwards.

Place the pot in the shade.

Wait for a new plant to sprout from the base of the leaf together with roots. Once the initial leaf has withered away, remove the new plant and repot in a pot filled with potting compost.

PROPAGATING FROM CRASSULA OVATA

Take a 10-cm (4-in) cutting from a mature plant at a joint using a clean knife.

Either dip the cutting in rooting hormone powder and leave to dry, or place it in a transparent jar of water.

Wait until roots form, then place in a small pot of free-draining compost (see page 182).

PROPAGATING FROM OPUNTIA OR OTHER SEGMENTED PLANTS

Detach a mature leaf pad from the body of the plant by making a clean cut with a sharp knife.

Leave in a cool, dry place for two weeks for a callous to form over the cut end.

Place the cut end of the pad in a pot filled to a depth of 1cm (½in) with free-draining compost (see page 182).

Wait for two weeks before watering.

STYLING

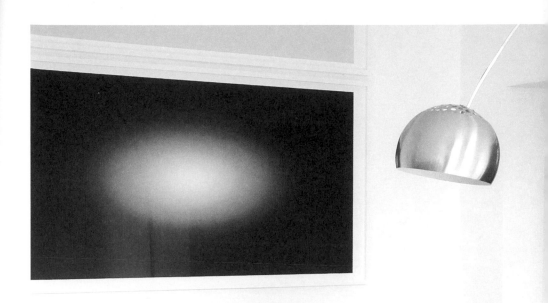

STYLING

As a cactus and succulent lover, my dream would be to have a garden like this one I stumbled across in California. I could come home to this garden every day and see it flourish and grow straight out of the earth. Unfortunately, I, like many others, do not live in these gorgeous climates. What's more, I am a city dweller and don't even have a garden, which means it's even more important to bring the green indoors. Most homes are warm and dry and have several bright areas – perfect for cacti and succulents to thrive. Together with their low-maintenance requirements and toughness, these plants are the perfect addition to the modern home.

And they needn't be restricted to the windowsill, although they can look very nice there…. With a little imagination, you can use them to transform different spaces in your home, while bringing out the very best of the plants as you do so. In this section I will outline some of my favourite ways to achieve exactly that.

FEATURE WALL

An empty wall or bookshelf can be transformed by a collection of contrasting cacti and succulents in an array of pots, hangers and bowls. You can use symmetry or just random positioning; it's the large number of plants that is key to making this feature a success. The result is an eclectic and rustic feel. Make sure to choose a wall that is flooded with natural light and have fun adding to this feature over time, perhaps swapping plants periodically to keep the display interesting.

NEGATIVE SPACE

There are areas in the home that are referred to as "negative space" because they are empty and awkward to fill. You can easily convert any such void with a collection of cacti and succulents in a variety of heights and textures. I love to use pots of the same colour to achieve a minimal look and also provide some synergy. This is a perfect way to fill an empty fireplace or space in front of one side of a patio door.

PLANT ARCHITECTURE

When they are placed in the home, large plants are transformed into pieces of art. They become modern, living sculptures. These can be in the form of a solo tall, statuesque cactus or large, impressive bowls of clumping *Mammillaria*, or a solitary, barrel-shaped cactus. The onus is on the size and impact of the plant in the room to produce the wow factor required from a statement piece.

The following are just a few examples of cacti and succulents that make wonderful (and tall) statement pieces in the home:

Cereus (see page 50)

Cleistocactus (see page 54)

Euphorbia (see page 85)

Large clumping *Mammillaria* (see page 118)

Mature *Astrophytum ornatum* (see page 42)

PLANT STANDS

Plant stands are a creative way to introduce a range of heights. They can hold individual plants or you can use a shelf ladder to elevate a whole collection. They're also good for homes with underfloor heating, where the heat would seep into the compost of floor-standing plants, confusing their seasonal rhythm. For a more casual look, try finding some old, unused stools to use.

BATHROOM

The bathroom is usually a low-light, high-humidity area in the home and so not well suited to most cacti and succulents, which prefer dry air. But there are some notable exceptions – *Aloe vera* and *Sansevieria* – that can bring a touch of the outdoors to your daily routine.

Aloe vera (see page 37) positively thrives in humid, low-light conditions, while *Sansevieria* (see page 150), although preferring bright light and low humidity, is a most accommodating plant and will do well in a bathroom. Not only does *Sansevieria* add height and texture to a room that can be quite sterile in feel, it also absorbs toxins, such as nitrogen oxide and formaldehyde, which occur in a number of products found in the bathroom. Some followers of feng shui believe that the upward-pointing leaves of these plants reverse the negativity associated with the flushing motion of the toilet.

VERTICAL SPACE

When you have exhausted all windowsills and shelves, you should look upwards to exploit vertical space. A macramé hanger with a well-chosen plant can easily become the main feature of a room. Hangers look best positioned in front of a window or in the corner of a room beside a window.

My favourite hanging and cascading plants include:

Senecio rowleyanus (string of pearls – see page 161): these work well placed either in a hanger or simply on a shelf, with their stems flowing over the edge.

Any *Rhipsalis* cactus (see pages 148–149).

Any *Epiphyllum* cactus, but especially *E. anguliger* (fishbone cactus – see page 81).

Sedum morganianum (burro's tail – see page 154).

CENTREPIECE

You can create a bowl of succulents or cacti that blend and contrast to produce a wonderful centrepiece for a table or sideboard. It is best to group together plants that require similar care – mixing sunlight and watering requirements is going to make life difficult. Water will need to drain so that it doesn't pool and stagnate. This can be achieved by drilling a hole in the bottom of the bowl or by adding a layer of gravel, crocks, pebbles, grit or hydroponic stones to absorb water.

GLASS GARDEN

Beautiful glass terrariums can be used
for growing and displaying cacti and
succulents. Remember not to use the closed
type of terrarium, where the plants are
sealed inside, as the environment is too
wet for most of these plants to survive.
Add a layer of gravel to the terrarium first,
followed by a layer of activated charcoal
(to ward off bacteria), and then add the
compost, into which your succulents are
planted. The compost can, in turn, be
covered in gravel or sand, depending on
the look you want to achieve.

LIVING ROCK DISH

As well as bringing them indoors, you can also use succulents to style your garden. Any *Sempervivum* (see page 156) or *Sedum* (see page 154) can be grown outside all year round in window planters, or by using part of a broken planter, as shown here – a great, sustainable and very natural-looking technique for styling your plants outdoors.

GLOSSARY

areole
the raised, or sunken, part of a cactus from which its spines grow

basal
relating to the base of the plant, as in basal rosette

cactus
any spiny succulent plant belonging to the plant family Cataceae

chlorophyll
the green pigment in leaves used for photosynthesis

crocks
drainage material, such as broken pieces of terracotta, lining the bottom of a pot

cultivar
the named variety of a plant, such as 'Rubra', with distinct characteristics that have been bred or selected by growers

epiphyte (*adj.* epiphytic)
a plant that grows on another plant but not parasitically

f. (*in full* forma)
the part of a plant's name that indicates minor variations from the species, as in *Cereus repandus* f. *monstrosa*

genus (*plural* genera)
a group of closely related plants; in a plant's scientific name, the genus comes first, as in *Euphorbia canariensis*

globose
spherical in shape

glochid
a short, hair-like spine, often barbed

habit
a plant's method of growth or general appearance

hybrid
a plant created by cross-pollinating two different species or varieties, indicated by the symbol "×" in a plant's name

hydroponic stones
soilless growing medium for plants

inflorescence
the part of the plant that carries the flowers

John Innes compost
soil-based compost, available in four formulae, for the different stages of plant growth

obovate
egg-shaped, with the narrow end at the base

obtuse
with a rounded or blunt tip

offset
baby plant produced on the original parent plant, which can be removed to make a separate plant

pendent
hanging

photosynthesis
the process by which a plant turns sunlight into energy, enabling it to grow

polyhedral leaf
a solid leaf with four or more faces
made up of flat polygons

pumice
lightweight, porous volcanic rock,
added to compost to help provide
additional drainage

raceme
a single-stemmed inflorescence with
flowers growing on individual stalks
along the stem; the bottom flowers
open first as the raceme lengthens

rib
a ridge on the stem of a cactus

rooting hormone
usually a powder, applied to the
base of a cutting before planting, to
stimulate growth so that the roots
develop more quickly

rosette
a dense whorl of leaves, usually formed
at ground level

species
the specific unit within a genus; in
a plant's scientific name, the species
comes second, as in *Euphorbia
canariensis*

striation
slender, parallel, longitudinal grooves
or stripes on a plant

subsp. (*in full* subspecies)
part of a plant's scientific name
denoting a distinct variant of the main

species, as in *Crassula arborescens*
subsp. *undulatifolia*

substrate
the material in which a plant grows,
such as compost

succulent
any plant that is able to live in arid or
salty regions through water stored in
its fleshy leaves

syn. (*in full* synonym)
the part of a plant's name that indicates
an incorrect but often used alternative
name, as in *Cylindropuntia spinosior*
(syn. *Opuntia spinosior*)

terete
smooth and usually cylindrical and
tapering

trichome
a hair-like growth from a plant

tubercle (*adj.* tuberculate)
a small, wart-like nodule on the surface
of a plant

variegated
leaves marked with multiple colours

var. (*in full* varietas)
the part of a plant's name that indicates
a slight variation in the species'
structure, e.g. *Tephrocactus articulatus*
var. *papyracanthus*

BIBLIOGRAPHY

Anderson, Edward F. 2001. *The Cactus Family*.

Baldwin, Debra Lee. 2013. *Succulents Simplified*.

Britton, N.L. & Rose, J.N. 1919–1923. *Cactaceae: Descriptions and Illustrations of Plants of the Cactus Family*, Vols. 1–4.

Dortort, Fred. 2011. *The Timber Press Guide to Succulent Plants of the World*.

Eggli, Urs & Newton, Leonard E. 2010. *Etymological Dictionary of Succulent Plant Names*.

Grantham, Keith & Klaassen, Paul. 1999. *The Plantfinder's Guide to Cacti & Other Succulents*.

Higgins, Vera. 1956. *Cacti for Decoration*.

Leese, Sir Oliver. 1973. *Cacti*.

Mace, Tony & Mace, Suzanne. 2001. *Cacti and Succulents* (Hamlyn Care Manual).

McMillan, A.J.S. & Horobin, J.F. 1995. *Christmas Cacti – The Genus Schlumbergera and Its Hybrids*.

Perl, Philip. 1978. *The Time-Life Encyclopedia of Gardening – Cacti and Succulents*.

Pilbeam, John. 1984. *How to Care for Your Cacti*.

Pilbeam, John. 1984. *The Instant Guide to Healthy Succulents*.

Preston-Mafham, Ken. 2007. *500 Cacti – Species and Varieties in Cultivation*.

Preston-Mafham, Rod & Preston-Mafham, Ken. 1995. *Cacti – The Illustrated Dictionary*.

Rowley, Gordon. 1978. *The Illustrated Encyclopedia of Succulents*.

Rowley, Gordon. 1997. *A History of Succulent Plants*.

Rowley, Gordon. 2006. *Teratopia – The World of Cristate and Variegated Succulents*.

Schulz & Kapitany. 2005. *Echeveria Cultivars*.

Schulz, Rudolf. 2009. *Haworthia – For the Collector*.

Schuster, Danny. 1992. *The World of Cacti*.

Scott, S.H. 1958. *The Observer's Book of Cacti and Other Succulents*.

Subik, Rudolf. 1971. *Decorative Cacti – A Guide to Succulent House Plants*.

Van Laren, A.J. 1934. *Succulents, Other Than Cacti*.

WEBSITES

www.cactiguide.com
www.cactus-art.biz
www.iucnredlist.org
www.rhs.org.uk
www.theplantlist.org
www.worldofsucculents.com

SUPPLIERS & THANKS

Ceramic pots
GRØN atölye
Lazy Glaze
Lisa Ommanney
Make & Matter
Mickwitz Waldemarsson
Terracotta "Prick Pots"

Plant hangers
Huiswerk

Terrariums
Tiny Kingdom

Home owners/plant collectors
Aykut Diricanli
Benny Blanco
Dewbien Plummer
Fausto Merilio Morell
Ducós
Laxmi Hussain
Lim Khaw
Mary Lam
Matilda Egere-Coope

Additional picture credits
22–23 Private Collection/
Photo © Christie's Images/
Bridgeman Images
25 Florilegius/SSPL/Getty
Images
223 Kieran Pharaoh

INDEX

INDEX

ABOUT THE AUTHOR

Prick is the brainchild of Gynelle Leon, an award-winning photographer with a background that includes a forensic science MSc as well as careers in finance and fraud prevention (while simultaneously working on art and design projects). As Gynelle's passion for plant life began to take over, she decided to take up part-time work in floristry to learn the trade. This is Gynelle's first solo business venture, and she hopes to encourage a plant revolution by educating the masses about the benefits of living with plants, as well as sharing knowledge on how to keep them alive.

ACKNOWLEDGEMENTS

I would like to thank my Mother and Father for living with so many of plants, taking good care of my greenhouse and supporting me in every way.

Ike Okolie, for being my number one, my motivation, my support and my love.

Yewande Peace, for being such an inspiring woman in every way and an incredible best friend, even on the other side of the Atlantic Ocean.

Heather Sommerfield, for being my cactus road trip sidekick.

Jonathan Devo and Paul Lewis, for assisting me in photography.

Octopus Publishing, for making this book happen.

Special thanks go to:

Tony Irons, Collins Dalphinis, Laura Olson, The British Cactus and Succulent Society and my branch of Havering, for their continual support, expertise and knowledge. The RHS Lindley Library and its staff for helping me source so much information.

All the explorers, enthusiasts and botanists that have come before me and worked tirelessly in the quest for knowledge, producing incredible books and art that have fuelled my interest in and understanding of the subject. Especially Gordon Rowley and Len Newton.

Last, but not least, the creator of these incredible and wondrous plants!

PICTURE CREDITS

pp.22–23 Private Collection/ Photo © Christie's Images/ Bridgeman Images

p.25 Florilegius/SSPL/Getty Images